THE BEST OF GOD IS IN THE SMALL STUFF

= BRUCE & STAN =

BARBOUR

PUBLISHING

Published by Barbour Publishing, Inc., P.O. Box 719, Uhrichsville, Ohio 44683, www.barbourbooks.com

Our mission is to publish and distribute inspirational products offering exceptional value and biblical encouragement to the masses.

Member of the
Evangelical Christian
Publishers Association

Printed in the United States of America.

—CONTENTS—

Introduction 7

from *God Is in the Small Stuff. . .and It All Matters*

1. Understand the Nature of God 11
2. Get to Know God Better 13
3. Realize That God Loves You 15
4. You Can Know God's Will 18
5. Give God Time 21
6. Prayer: The Great Connector 23
7. Discipline Yourself (No One Else Will) . . 25
8. Improve Yourself (No One Else Can) . . . 27
9. Your Body Is a Temple 30
10. Simplify Life and Enjoy It More 32
11. Arrange Your Priorities 35
12. Contentment Is Good for the Soul 38
13. Stop Worrying and Start Living 40
14. The God Who Comforts Us 42
15. Communication Is More Than Talking . . 44
16. Encouragement Is a Gift 47
17. Money: Learn to Deal with It 49
18. A Generous Spirit Works Wonders 52
19. Laugh and the World Laughs with You . . 54
20. Relationships Take Time 56
21. You Need Your Friends 58
22. *Carpe Diem*: Seize the Day 61
23. God Is in the Small Stuff 63

from *God Is in the Small Stuff for Your Marriage*

24. Love and Marriage. 69
25. Dating Doesn't Stop with the Wedding. . . 73
26. Finding Occasions to Celebrate 76
27. Making Time for Your Spouse 79
28. Speaking a Language Your Spouse
    Understands 81
29. Let God Come between You 84
30. Reading the Marriage Manual 86
31. God Knows What Your Marriage Needs . . 89
32. Opposites Attract. 91
33. Seasons of Marriage 93
34. The Joy of Becoming 96
35. When and How Many. 98
36. Parenting 101 101
37. The Care and Coaching of Teenagers . . 104
38. No Kids? Know Kids! 106
39. You Married an Entire Family. 108
40. Love Thy Neighbor 111
41. Fiscal Intimacy. 114
42. Yours, Mine, and Ours 116
43. Time, Pressure, and Fatigue 119
44. Vacations Are Supposed to Be a
    Waste of Time 122
45. The True Meaning of Love 125
46. Your Marriage Is Your Greatest Legacy . . 127

from *God Is in the Small Stuff for Your Family*

47. Heritage 131
48. Traditions. 134

49. Hospitality 137
50. God 140
51. Church. 143
52. Stewardship. .147
53. Humor. 150
54. Travel 153
55. Marriage. 156
56. Teenagers 159
57. Grandparents and Grandchildren 163
58. Family Reunions 166
59. Working Parents 169
60. Letting Go 172
61. Crisis 176
62. Divorce. 179
63. Education. 182
64. Money Management. 184
65. Responsibilities 187
66. Encouragement. 190
67. Discipline 193
68. Authority 196
69. Decision Making 199

from *God Is in the Small Stuff for Tough Times*

70. "Why, God, Why?" 205
71. Innocent Suffering 209
72. When Life Doesn't Seem Fair 212
73. Where Is God When We Suffer? 215
74. You're Not Exempt 218
75. Thanking God. 222
76. The Story of Job 226

77. When Prayer Doesn't Seem to Work. . . . 230

78. How to Know God's Will 234

79. When Children Turn Away. 237

80. Caring for Aging Parents 240

81. The Long Good-Bye 244

82. From Busted to Belief 248

83. A Loss of Self 252

84. Giving to God. 256

85. Confronted with Cancer 260

86. Does God Still Heal?. 264

87. Hearing God. 267

88. When Children Suffer 271

89. Going from Hurting to Healing 275

90. Will Your Pet Be in Heaven?. 278

91. Afraid to Death of Dying 282

92. God Is in the Small Stuff for
    Tough Times 286

from *God Is in the Small Stuff at Christmas*

93. God's Story. 293

94. The Coming Messiah. 296

95. Hope 300

96. Faith. 304

97. Prepare Him Room 307

98. Joy 310

99. Gifts and Giving 313

100. Receiving 316

About the Authors 319

A few years ago we wrote a book called *God Is in the Small Stuff...and It All Matters.* That book has helped millions of people understand that God delights in the details of their lives (Psalm 37:23). In a world where natural disasters, political unrest, economic pressures, and conflicts over marriage cry out for our attention, it's tempting to ask, "Where is God in all of this?"

Some are quick to blame God for all the troubles in the world. We want to suggest a different approach. Now more than ever, we are convinced that people need to be reassured that God isn't detached or disinterested in what's going on. Just the opposite. As the Bible says, "God is our refuge and strength, always ready to help in times of trouble" (Psalm 46:1 NLT).

In addition to the original *God Is in the Small Stuff* book, we've written several others that show just how much God cares about us in every detail in our lives, our marriages, our families, when times are good, and especially during tough times. The book you are holding represents the best of all our God Is in the Small Stuff volumes. We have carefully selected topics from each book we believe are relevant and helpful to what you may be experiencing right now.

The selections from *God Is in the Small Stuff...and It All Matters* are intended to help you learn to know God better. As you read them, we hope you come to understand that God wants you to invite Him into every detail of your life.

We chose the chapters from *God Is in the Small Stuff*

for Your Marriage to offer the positive message that God values marriage and wants to be involved in this sacred relationship.

Families are incredibly important to God. After all, He sent His only Son, Jesus Christ, to be born into a family. As our heavenly Father, God loves us as if we were His own children—which we are! We hope this message comes across in the chapters we have selected from *God Is in the Small Stuff for Your Family*.

Not every day is a good day, and many of our readers struggle with the everyday burdens and cares of life. That's why we wrote *God Is in the Small Stuff for Tough Times*. We wanted to affirm that God knows what you are going through, and He wants to give you the help you need to endure the troubles of life.

Finally, we hope the few essays we have chosen from *God Is in the Small Stuff at Christmas* will help you understand that the tradition of Christmas, which we all cherish each year, is the greatest story ever told—when God personally entered our world so we could personally relate to Him in every circumstance.

Whether you read this compilation straight through, or start with the section that is most meaningful to you right now, we hope you find these 100 chapters to be an encouragement for your own spiritual journey. Even more, we pray that you will connect with God in a more meaningful way as you begin to see Him in the small stuff of your life.

Bruce & Stan

—from—

God Is in the Small Stuff. . .
and It All Matters

Do you not know? Have you not heard?
The LORD is the everlasting God,
the Creator of the ends of the earth.
He will not grow tired or weary,
and his understanding no one can fathom.
ISAIAH 40:28 NIV

= I =

UNDERSTAND THE NATURE OF GOD

Who is God? Is He a mystery to you? Do you want to know Him better? Maybe you wonder if God even exists. That's okay. People have wondered about God for as long as. . .well, for as long as there have been people. They wonder if He's really out there. They wonder if He made the world and everything in it. And if He did, they wonder if God still cares about what's going on.

Perhaps you've gotten past all of those questions. You definitely believe in God, but you don't know Him. You don't understand His nature—in other words, His personality. You aren't alone. For many people—even those who claim to be religious—the nature of God is a mystery. It's like God is behind some dark cloud, occasionally speaking in a deep voice to prophets and such (you know, like He spoke to Charlton Heston in *The Ten Commandments*). Other people think God wants to prevent them from having a good time. If they get close to God, they're afraid they'll have to give up their freedom.

While it's true there are things about God we'll never know (after all, He is God), there are many things we *can* know. For example, when we look at our universe—whether it's through a microscope, a telescope, or the naked eye—we observe incredible design and order and beauty. That means the Designer (that would be God) must be a Being of design and order and beauty. And He must be pretty powerful.

When we look at ourselves and see that we all have some idea about God (even when you deny God exists, you have to think about Him), that means the Creator (God again) put that idea in us. Yet God is more than an idea. He is more than a symbol for good or an impersonal "higher being." God is a very real spirit Being who has always existed in the past, who exists now, and who will always exist in the future. God is personal. God is involved in our world. And God has revealed His nature to us. All we have to do is stop, look, and listen.

. . .In the Small Stuff

- God will never send a thirsty soul to a dry well.
- God is more likely to speak to you with a gentle whisper than with a loud voice.
- The times when you need God the most are when you don't think you need Him.

Then the way you live will always honor
and please the Lord. . . . All the while, you will
learn to know God better and better.
COLOSSIANS 1:10 NLT

= 2 =

GET TO KNOW GOD BETTER

Does God seem distant? Is He detached from you? Maybe that's because you are waiting for God to come to you. If so, then you've got things backward.

God has given us His Word, His Son, and His Spirit. That is more than we will ever need in order to understand God (and certainly more than we can absorb in a lifetime). But the next step belongs to each of us. It's up to us to read God's Word, to believe in His Son, and to follow the guidance of the Holy Spirit.

You see, God is a perfect gentleman. He never forces Himself on anyone. He anxiously desires a deep and meaningful personal relationship with you, but He won't force the issue. It must be voluntary on your part. So, if you want to get to know God better, *you* must approach *Him*. When

Jesus taught about this principle, He presented the relationship as an invitation:

> *Look! Here I stand at the door and knock. If you hear me calling and open the door, I will come in, and we will share a meal as friends.*
>
> REVELATION 3:20 NLT

God makes Himself available, but you must respond to His invitation. Take Him at His Word. Go to Him. Open the door of your heart to Him.

You don't have to move to a monastery to know God better. You don't have to learn ancient Hebrew or memorize the names of the twelve disciples in alphabetical order. All it takes is your time and attention—reading His Word and talking to Him. Start with a few minutes each day, and grow from there. You don't have to call to schedule an appointment. He has already extended the invitation, and He's waiting for you to respond.

. . . IN THE SMALL STUFF

- Rather than worry about what you don't know about God, concentrate on what you do know.

- You begin to seek God for who He is when you stop seeking Him for what He can do for you.

- Have a passion for God and compassion for people.

This is real love.
It is not that we loved God, but that he loved us.
1 JOHN 4:10 NLT

= 3 =

REALIZE THAT GOD LOVES YOU

L ove is a powerful emotion, perhaps the strongest of human emotions. People will go to great lengths to express love, and they will do almost anything to get love. So if love is in such demand, why does it seem in such short supply? To paraphrase the song, "Why is love the only thing that there's just too little of?"

The problem with human love is that it's usually self-centered. Much of the so-called love we feel could be summarized by the phrase, "What's in it for me?" We may think we love someone, but in reality we may simply love what he or she does for us.

The great writer C. S. Lewis identified four different kinds of love, all but one of which are basically self-centered. First, there's *affection*, which is the kind of love we can have for something other than people, such as a dog or a home or a car. Then there's *friendship*, a valuable love in the sense that it's the basis of most human relationships. And there's *erotic* love, which is beautiful between a husband and wife but a mess outside of married love. All of these are wonderful and necessary loves, but each of them depends on the object of our affection for complete fulfillment.

The only love that is completely other-centered is called *agape* love. This is love of the highest order. It's what Lewis called "Divine Gift-Love." When we love with *agape* love, we desire the best for the people we love. We are even able to love those who are unlovable.

We are capable of *agape* love only to the extent that we give the details of our lives over to God and allow Him to work in us. But even before that can happen, we must realize that God loves us, and that He can only love us with this kind of love. God's love is never self-centered, and God's love is always sacrificial. While we were enemies of God, He loved us. When we ran from God, He loved us. And He loved us so much that He sacrificed the Son He loved most so that we could experience eternal life.

Love is the essence of God. Love is what motivates Him to do what He does for us—down to the last detail—even when we don't love Him in return. Knowing that should give tremendous meaning to our lives.

- Whenever you feel insignificant, remember how important you are to God.

- We love God because we know who He is. God loves us despite who we are.

- God's unconditional love for us should motivate us to love others unconditionally.

"If you believe, you will receive whatever you ask for in prayer."
MATTHEW 21:22 NLT

= 4 =

YOU CAN KNOW GOD'S WILL

God's will is a paradox. It's both easy to find and difficult to discern. God's will can be immediate, or it may take years to figure out. God's will can frustrate you or give you tremendous peace.

One thing is for sure. You *can* know God's will. Although it may seem mysterious, there's really no mystery to it. If you know where to look, God's will is there. And if you listen carefully, God will speak to you in amazing ways.

First of all, God speaks through His Word, the Bible. Everything we need for living a life that pleases God—and what could be more in His will than that?—is in the Bible. As you get to know God's Word, you will get to know God's will.

Second, God speaks through your own judgment and common sense. But beware. Your decisions will line up with God's will only if you know God personally in the first place, and then only if your relationship with God is right. When you're in this condition, you will operate with "the mind of Christ." The Holy Spirit will guide you from the inside.

Finally, and most commonly, God speaks through the details of your life. Oswald Chambers put it this way: "God speaks in the language you know best—not through your ears but through your circumstances."

You think your life is an accident? Not a chance. You're here for a reason. And what you do matters to God. Everything. Not just the stuff you do in church or Bible study (although that is very important), but in the everyday small stuff. That's where you'll find God's will most often.

Take a look at your life. Think about the moments and events—the details—and see how far you've come. Those "good things" weren't coincidences. You weren't just "lucky." If your heart has followed after God, then God has been leading you, and you have been doing His will, perhaps without even knowing it.

On the other hand, if you feel like life is dealing you one bad hand after another, and you feel sorry for yourself—and you're mad at God—maybe it's time to get back to basics. Take the focus off of yourself and get to know God better by reading His Word, praying, and associating with people who are in God's will. God wants to direct you through the details of your life. Give Him a chance.

- Don't make plans and then ask for the Lord's approval. Ask God to direct your planning.

- Remember that God's will is not so much a function of time and place as it is an attitude of the heart.

- Circumstances may be outside your control, but the way you respond to them is not.

Be still in the presence of the LORD,
and wait patiently for him to act.
PSALM 37:7 NLT

= 5 =

GIVE GOD TIME

If there's one thing we need in the midst of our busy, loud, and nervous lives, it's the inner peace and quiet and assurance that only God can give. It's the only way to see God's purposes for us, let alone keep our sanity.

The thing is, God doesn't yell out and say, "Hey, you're neglecting Me. Sit still for a moment so you can hear Me." Oh, He is fully capable of getting our attention when we really need it, but you don't want to make a habit of giving God a reason to chase you down (and He will).

Rather than waiting for God to whack you over the head with a spiritual two-by-four, wouldn't it be far better to give God some time each day to quietly speak to you? Actually, this is God's preference. "Be silent, and know that I am God!" He says (Psalm 46:10 NLT). Being still may be the hardest thing you will ever do, but it may be the most important. Look at it this way. When you give God time, you show Him respect. In effect you're saying, "God, You're important enough to me to set aside some time each day. I want You to teach me, and I want to learn."

Will God talk to you if you let Him? Most definitely. Not in an audible voice, but through your thoughts and emotions. God also talks through His Word, the Bible. Remember, the Bible is God's voice for us. The only way to hear it is to read it.

The doorway to letting God into the details of your life—into your concerns and dreams—is time. We know this won't be easy. Many other voices will call out for your time and attention, and many of them are worthwhile. But if you want to hear the one Voice who will make all the difference in your life, you'll need to let God in. . .quietly.

Ask God to give you the desire to set aside a place and a time just for Him. The details of your life will wait. More than that, they'll take on more meaning when you give them over to God.

. . .In the Small Stuff

- The advantage of meeting God at the same time each day is that you don't have to decide when you are going to do it.

- Rising early to meet the Lord gives you a jump on the day. Meeting God at night enables you to reflect on the day. Either option is good.

- The time to find moments of stillness and quiet is when it's the most difficult to do so.

The eyes of the Lord watch over those who do right,
and his ears are open to their prayers.

1 PETER 3:12 NLT

= 6 =

PRAYER: THE GREAT CONNECTOR

One day the disciples requested of Jesus: "Teach us to pray." Jesus responded by giving them—and us—a marvelous model of prayer. What is so powerful about the Lord's Prayer, as it is known, is its utter simplicity.

> *Our Father in heaven, may your name be honored.*
> *May your Kingdom come soon. May your will be done*
> *here on earth, just as it is in heaven. Give us our food*
> *for today, and forgive us our sins, just as we have for-*
> *given those who have sinned against us. And don't let*
> *us yield to temptation, but deliver us from the evil one.*
> MATTHEW 6:9–13 NLT

The key to prayer is to start simply and quietly. That's the idea behind Jesus' model prayer. We need a touchstone, a place to start. Then, as we get to know God better, we will feel comfortable sharing the most intimate details of our lives with Him.

If the Bible is God talking to us, then prayer is us talking to God. It's the primary way of connecting to the infinite, all-powerful, all-knowing, all-loving God. Edward Ferrell wrote that "without prayer, there is no way, no truth, no life." Without prayer, you can never get close to God.

Try it. Start small. Start with the small stuff in your life. Talk to God about it in a quiet, isolated place where your self-consciousness isn't an issue. As you continue daily, your capacity for prayer will grow larger. That's because prayer is like a muscle. If you exercise it regularly, your prayer muscle will gain strength and your appreciation for God will grow immeasurably. On the other hand, if you don't use it, your prayer muscle will shrivel up and your capacity for God will shrink. And in those times of crisis when you suddenly feel compelled to pray, it will likely be a painful experience.

The good news is that God doesn't put conditions on your prayer life. His feelings don't get hurt when you don't pray. But when you do, He connects with you in a powerful way. Try it today. Try it right now. Talk to God. He's listening.

. . .IN THE SMALL STUFF

- Prayer without effort will be insincere. Effort without prayer will be ineffective.
- If your prayers don't mean anything to you, they mean even less to God.
- Prayer involves listening to God as well as speaking to Him.

To learn, you must love discipline.
PROVERBS 12:1 NLT

= 7 =

DISCIPLINE YOURSELF (NO ONE ELSE WILL)

Humans are funny beings. It used to be that many of us wanted every material thing we could get our hands on, and we wanted whatever it was to be bigger, better, or faster. Then we discovered that *outward* material things don't make us happy. So over the last few years we've turned *inward*. We've decided that it's what's inside that counts. Consequently, many of us have embarked on an inward journey, seeking to simplify our lifestyles while increasing our joy. At least that's the goal, because that's what the simplicity gurus are telling us in books like *Simple Abundance* and *Living the Simple Life*.

The idea of simplifying your life is a good one, and we'll talk more about that in chapter 10. The problem is that we are attacking the goal with the same unbridled zest we used to collect all that stuff in the first place. Like a crazy pendulum, we swing from one extreme to the other with gusto, somehow feeling empty at both places.

So how do you find the satisfaction you've been looking for? The key is balance, consistency, and perseverance, all of which come from one thing and one thing only: *discipline.*

Here's our dilemma. We want it all, and we want it now, whether it's an abundance of possessions or an abundance of simplicity. But nothing worthwhile comes quickly, and nothing worthwhile comes without discipline. Over life's long haul, discipline works in every dimension of your life: financial, physical, mental, and spiritual. If you've ever tried to get rich quick, tried to lose weight by taking a pill, tried to get knowledge by cramming at the last minute, or attempted to get close to God by asking for a miracle, you know what we're talking about.

It's easy to get caught in the trap of quick results when you focus on the results rather than the journey. The truth is, the joy is in the journey, in the daily discipline of growing in the details of your mind, body, and spirit. The only way to bring abundance to your life—the kind of abundance that gives you joy—is to bring discipline into your life.

. . .IN THE SMALL STUFF

- Discipline begins with small things done daily.
- Don't be good at making excuses.
- People will be more impressed by what you finish than by what you start.

No, dear friends, I am still not all I should be,
but I am focusing all my energies on this one thing:
Forgetting the past and looking forward
to what lies ahead...

PHILIPPIANS 3:13 NLT

= 8 =

IMPROVE YOURSELF (NO ONE ELSE CAN)

Will there ever be a time when you will stop learning and improving yourself? Will it happen when you get your high school diploma? Not then, because the education process has only just begun. At college graduation? Hardly, because the lessons of the real world await. When you become a parent with your own children to raise? Certainly not, because every parent has to stay mentally sharp just to keep up with the "new math." Will you be able to stop learning and improving when you reach your "golden years"? That's doubtful, because then you'll need more wits than ever to figure out all of the discounts to which you are entitled.

So when does your quest to improve yourself end?

When you stop breathing. Between now and then, you should consider *yourself* to be an ongoing project. A work in process. Always improving. Never stagnant.

Self-improvement is a popular topic. In the midst of our current technology generation, we are told that our minds are like computers—they are only as good as they are programmed. But the emphasis on continuing personal development is not unique to contemporary society. Several decades ago someone wrote, "You are what you think." And even before that, the Bible said, "For as he thinketh in his heart, so is he" (Proverbs 23:7 kjv).

God did not design you to be stagnant or sluggish in any respect: spiritually, physically, mentally, or socially. To borrow a book title from Chuck Swindoll, God intends that you "live above the level of mediocrity."

Self-improvement doesn't happen automatically. It requires constant, systematic, and disciplined personal development. There are books to be read, people to meet, and new places to discover. Your personal growth is a privilege, not a burden. This is where God loves to get involved in the details of your life. Let Him in and watch Him work in the small stuff of your life to help you grow and improve.

Each day, as you begin again your process of personal growth, remember that it all begins with your attitude. You must prepare your heart and program your mind for self-improvement. Like the Scripture says, "Fix your thoughts on what is true and honorable and right. Think about things that are pure and lovely and admirable. Think about things that are excellent and worthy of praise" (Philippians 4:8 nlt).

- Learn from the mistakes of others. You'll never live long enough to make them all yourself.

- Don't take pride in exceeding your expectations if your goals were only mediocre.

- Never mistake activity for achievement.

Don't you know that your body is the temple
of the Holy Spirit, who lives in you
and was given to you by God?
1 Corinthians 6:19 nlt

= 9 =

YOUR BODY IS A TEMPLE

One of the great mysteries of our culture can be found in our obsession with physical fitness. The mystery isn't that people are exercising more. The mystery is that we're in worse shape than ever.

With the proliferation of fitness clubs, the emphasis on eating healthy foods, and the presence of at least three late-night cable shows dedicated to the latest home exercise apparatus, we should be the fittest people on the planet. Unfortunately, *should* never got anybody into shape.

The sad truth is that we are gaining weight at an alarming rate, our children are in terrible shape, and even our professional athletes get beaten by athletes from other countries in any sport we didn't first invent.

What's the problem? We think it has to do with *intention* and *attention*. You probably have every *intention* of getting fit, but you don't. You say you're going to pay *attention* to the details of diet and exercise, but you don't. When you put those two failures together, they spell "out of shape." And out of shape usually leads to all kinds of disadvantages, such as shortness of breath, sleepiness, lack of endurance, and obesity—none of which will add years or quality to your life.

Just like every other area of your life, the secret to getting and staying healthy lies in the details. Change won't happen overnight. It takes time as a multitude of small disciplines are repeated daily. The process may be tedious, but the results are well worth the effort. Not only will you feel better, but you'll think better, too! A sound body can enhance a sound mind (conversely, health problems due to sloppy eating habits and sporadic exercise routines can undermine the mind).

We may be spiritual creatures at heart, but while we're on earth our spirits are being housed in our physical bodies. Let's do everything we can to keep the house in top shape.

. . .IN THE SMALL STUFF

- Fitness of the soul should take priority over fitness of the body, but the two are not mutually exclusive.
- A healthy body and a sharp mind usually go together.
- Run the race to win, even if you don't stand a chance.

*This should be your ambition: to live
a quiet life, minding your own business.*
1 THESSALONIANS 4:11 NLT

= 10 =

SIMPLIFY LIFE AND ENJOY IT MORE

Do you long for the simple life? Many people do. It seems as if we're all too busy, have too much stuff, and owe too many bills (mainly because we have too much stuff). If you've ever said to yourself, "Stop the world, I want to get off," then you're probably a good candidate for simplicity.

But what does that mean? You may hear the word *simplicity* and right away think of self-imposed poverty or lowered ambitions. You may think of the simple life as an empty, boring existence. Think again.

Simplicity doesn't take away from your life. A simpler lifestyle may actually *add* quality and contentment to your life. When it comes to life, simplicity doesn't mean poverty. Quite the opposite, when you identify those things and those people who are really important to you, your life takes on more meaning because you proactively choose to do those things that will increase the quality of your life. The net result is that your life is *richer*, not poorer.

For most of us, our problem isn't that we need *more*. What we need is *better*. Do you have any things you no longer use or wear because they no longer add value to your life? Get rid of them (give them to people who don't have any stuff). Is your schedule so overloaded that you don't have time for those people and those activities that add to your life rather than taking away from it? Learn how to say "no." Learn to prioritize.

While you're giving stuff away and learning to say no, keep this profound thought in mind: the reason our lives are so complicated is that we're too self-centered. Richard Foster writes that "simplicity means moving away from total absorption in ourselves. . .to being centered in. . .God."

God isn't the one who leads you to a more complicated life (and more stress). You get there quite well all by yourself. God wants you to give the small stuff and the stress of your life over to Him. When you trust God and let Him take the lead in your life, you will find that your life will be more peaceful and more productive. You will naturally want to clear out the clutter to make more room for God.

Thomas Kelly wrote that our deepest need "is not food and clothing and shelter, important as they are. It is God."

- Satisfaction begins when comparison stops.

- Your wealth is measured by the fewness of your wants.

- What you are bears little resemblance to what you have.

*"Your heavenly Father already knows all your needs,
and he will give you all you need from day to day
if you live for him and make the Kingdom
of God your primary concern."*
MATTHEW 6:32–33 NLT

= II =

ARRANGE YOUR PRIORITIES

Here's an exercise that will absolutely amaze you. At the end of a day (any old day will do), sit down with a blank piece of paper and write down everything you did that day. Everything. Every detail. If you're fairly thorough (and honest), you're going to end up with a list of more than a hundred items.

Now go back and rank your activities according to the following scale, which was developed by Richard Foster:

1 – Essential
2 – Important but not essential
3 – Helpful but not necessary
4 – Trivial

When you're done, look at your list. You will see two remarkable things. First, you'll notice how many details there are in one day. How did you do all of that? Second, you'll notice how much time you spent on unnecessary and trivial things, and how little time you spent on essential and important details. Assuming you were honest, you now have a measure of your priorities, and they may not be what you expected. You thought the essential and important things were the top priorities of your life, but it's the unnecessary and even the trivial things that occupy the majority of your time.

The trouble is that the details of our lives don't really amount to much when you look at them from God's perspective. It's not that God doesn't care about our small stuff. He cares more than we do. All He asks is that we put Him at the top of our priority list.

Jesus made a simple statement about priorities when He said, "Make the Kingdom of God your primary concern" (Matthew 6:33 NLT). What did He mean by this? Instead of being preoccupied with the details of your life, focus on God first. Trust Him to arrange your priorities. Trust Him to handle the small stuff.

When you reduce your priorities to one detail—and it's God—then every other detail falls into place. Not right away. If this is new to you, it's going to take some time. But in a relatively short time—if you stay at it every day and give the small stuff of your life over to God—you will have a clearer and more effective focus in your life.

- If what you are doing won't make a difference in five years, it probably doesn't matter now.

- You'll know something becomes meaningful when it goes from your head to your heart to your hands.

- Strive to be a person of faith rather than fame.

True religion with contentment is great wealth.
1 Timothy 6:6 nlt

= 12 =

CONTENTMENT IS GOOD FOR THE SOUL

Like so many words, we've lost the meaning of *content-ment*. We've somehow come up with the notion that contentment is the opposite of success. We believe contentment is attainable only if we stop striving, and who wants to do that? We're afraid that if we stand still for a moment, the world is going to pass us by, so we make up our minds that we'll be contented *someday*, perhaps when we retire.

If you're an average person trying to get ahead in the world, contentment is probably the last thing you're striving for, yet there's a good chance that you *long* for it. Why? Because at its core, contentment is peace of mind. Contentment is happiness. The person who is content has little or no stress.

Yet we forge ahead like a soldier going into battle. We dive headlong into society's raging river and get caught up in a cycle of overspending, overcommitting, and overworking.

And all for what? Happiness. Peace of mind. Satisfaction. But we're only kidding ourselves. Striving, consuming, and accumulating will never bring happiness. What they bring is anxiety, worry, unhappiness, and—in the long run—ineffectiveness.

Even as you read this, let your mind slow down and reflect on some qualities of true contentment. First of all, being content doesn't mean being lazy. Discontentment affects the rich and poor alike. What they have in common is that they both want more stuff.

Second, don't equate contentment with being lowly or meek. There is tremendous power in contentment, because when you are content with what you have, you are free. You are free from pretense, free from concern over having it all *now*, and (in most cases) free from stress.

Third, it's not only possible but desirable to be both content and ambitious. If your ambitions come from a desire to serve God, to help others, and to improve yourself so you will have a greater impact in your world, then the fulfillment of your ambitions will bring you much happiness and contentment.

. . .In the Small Stuff

- Don't acquire everything you want.
- Since exhaustion begins and ends on the inside, that's where genuine rest must originate.
- A good life is of more value than a good living.

"So I tell you, don't worry about everyday life—
whether you have enough food, drink, and clothes.
Doesn't life consist of more than food and clothing?"
MATTHEW 6:25 NLT

= 13 =

STOP WORRYING AND START LIVING

Worrying is one of the most destructive of all human habits because it decreases your effectiveness in other areas. When you worry about something, your thoughts and your emotions focus on events that haven't yet taken place. It's like Mark Twain once said: "I am an old man and have known a great many troubles, but most of them have never happened."

Worrying is totally passive. It accomplishes nothing. On the other hand, worrying can literally make you sick while keeping you from accomplishing the things that really matter. Here's a sobering thought: worry can keep you from living your life the way God intended it.

Think about the things you worry about. Amazingly, you probably worry about the small stuff. Those details of life over which you have little or no control. Oswald Chambers wrote: "It is not only wrong to worry, it is unbelief; worrying means we do not believe that God can look after the practical details of our lives, and it is never anything but those details that worry us."

Jesus asked the rhetorical question, "Can all your worries add a single moment to your life? Of course not" (Matthew 6:27 NLT). If anything, worries can and will take away from your life. Are you trying to arrange the details of your life so carefully that you are leaving God out of the process? Then you're probably worrying too much. You're relying on your own abilities, and you think you have a lot to lose if things don't turn out the way you want.

Clearly the antidote to worry is trusting God to take care of the small stuff of your life. Invite Him to get involved in the details of your life. "Give all your worries and cares to God," says the Bible, "for he cares about what happens to you" (1 Peter 5:7 NLT).

. . .IN THE SMALL STUFF

- Live longer by worrying less.
- Instead of worrying about what you can't do, think about what God can do for you.
- Never confuse worrying about tomorrow with planning for tomorrow.

He is the source of every mercy
and the God who comforts us.
2 CORINTHIANS 1:3 NLT

= 14 =

THE GOD WHO COMFORTS US

Comfort is a rare and wonderful gift. Do you remember a time when you were a kid and you badly needed some comfort? Perhaps it was something as simple as a skinned knee, but your mother took it seriously and gave you comfort by kissing and then bandaging the hurt and telling you everything would be all right. Or maybe as you got older and someone you cared about hurt you deeply, a friend comforted you with words of encouragement.

Such memories are warm and wonderful. Yet sometimes the comfort of a loved one isn't enough. Sometimes the hurt is so deep that no human words can help relieve the pain. No mere bandage can cover the damage.

That's when you need to look beyond human comfort

to something much more effective—the comfort of God. This isn't some mystical, faraway concept. God really does provide comfort to those who call upon Him in times of need. The trouble is that many people are so busy blaming God for their troubles that they don't even realize how close He is and how much He wants to comfort them. Unlike human comfort, which feels good for a moment, God's comfort supplies strength for a lifetime.

The meaning of comfort takes on significance when it describes God's actions toward us. When the Bible talks about God's comfort, it describes a comfort of strength and refreshment. At the root of God's comfort is the idea of nearness. Indeed, when He comforts us, God calls us near.

Is God calling you near in your time of trouble? Go to Him in prayer and through His Word. There you'll find strength, safety, and solace. Are you hurting? Do you struggle with loneliness? God wants you to draw near to Him so you can feel His overwhelming love. Go ahead. Ask God for His comfort in every detail of your life.

. . .In the Small Stuff

- God doesn't promise you a life without difficulties. But He does promise that He will always be with you.

- It is possible for God to give you comfort without removing your adversity.

- One of the reasons God comforts us is so that we can comfort others.

Dear friends, be quick to listen, slow to speak,
and slow to get angry.
JAMES 1:19 NLT

= 15 =

COMMUNICATION IS MORE THAN TALKING

When it comes to communication, there are two kinds of people in the world—those who love to hear others talk, and those who love to hear themselves talk (and we all know which kinds of people are more fun to be with).

Good communication skills begin with listening. Not only do you learn things about other people by listening, but you also make others feel important when you give them your full attention, complete with head nods and eye contact. Of course, your goal may be to help others become good listeners by doing all the talking yourself. While we don't recommend this, we do offer this word of advice: learn to distinguish between head nods that show genuine interest and those that indicate that your listener is dozing off out of sheer boredom.

If you're still not convinced that listening is a better communication skill than talking, try this experiment. The next time you're with a bunch of people at a party or special event, do your best to listen intently. Stroke your chin and say, "I see," when someone makes a point. Occasionally squint your eyes and go, "Mmmm," when another person says something interesting. Ask questions rather than make statements.

If you keep this up, we guarantee that at the end of the evening you will be considered by everyone else to be the most thoughtful and dynamic person in the room. You will also appear incredibly wise.

Even if you don't aspire to become a world-class listener, you can always improve your communication skills by self-editing your conversations. Keep talking, but use fewer words (*better* words, too). Avoid the extremes of empty flattery and harmful gossip (what other kind of gossip is there?).

Here's another form of nonverbal communication that's extremely effective. Whenever someone has done something nice for you, send a thank-you note. When someone needs a lift, write a personal note of encouragement. When tragedy strikes another, express your sympathy with a heartfelt card. You'll never know how meaningful your written words will be to others.

- A card sent with a personal note inside is more meaningful than a card sent but only signed.

- Listen with your eyes as well as your ears.

- No one will ever accuse you of being a boring conversationalist if you let people talk about themselves.

So encourage each other and build each other up.
1 THESSALONIANS 5:11 NLT

= 16 =

ENCOURAGEMENT IS A GIFT

People seldom think of encouragement as a gift because it seems so ordinary. But it isn't. Encouragement is actually quite rare (because it's seldom given), and it is valuable (because it's so meaningful to the recipient). In our humble opinion, encouragement makes the perfect gift, and here's why:

It's free. Encouraging someone requires absolutely no cash outlay. This doesn't mean there is no cost. It may cost you time, creativity, and thoughtfulness. But all of that is what makes encouragement so appreciated. It requires something from *you*, not just something from your wallet.

It requires no shopping. You don't have to make a trip to the mall for this gift. Many times the gift can be delivered from your home or office. Writing a note of support or making an encouraging phone call may be all that's necessary.

It doesn't have to be gift-wrapped. Attractive wrapping adds to the appeal of a gift, but none is needed with encouragement. It is beautiful all by itself.

It can be custom-designed. You don't have to worry about sizes. But you must still give some thought to making your gift of encouragement a perfect fit. You have to think about some details—what are the best words of comfort, motivation, or support the person needs to hear.

It doesn't require batteries. So many gifts require batteries as an energy source. Not so with encouragement. It creates energy all by itself. If you don't think so, just watch the increase in activity when you motivate someone with a kind and supportive comment.

It will last a lifetime. Think about it. What other gift could you give to a child that will have value years later? Encouragement can do just that. A little word can make a big difference, and the results can be life-changing.

Oh, there's one more thing about encouragement. No one ever gets too much of it. So don't be stingy. Give it often.

. . . In the Small Stuff

- You can't always control the kind of service you receive, but you can always control the kind of gratitude you deliver.

- Just as you can have false modesty, you can encourage insincerely. Learn to be a sincere encourager.

- Encourage those who look up to you.

= 17 =

MONEY: LEARN TO DEAL WITH IT

What is it about money that causes business partnerships to dissolve, friendships to break apart, and marriages to end? More accurately, what is it about money that motivates people to turn against each other?

As usual, the answer to this crucial question can be found in the Bible. Actually, money is a major topic in the Bible. Jesus frequently talked about money because He knew that its most damaging effect is to keep people away from God. He once said, "It is very hard for a rich person to get into the Kingdom of Heaven" (Matthew 19:23 NLT).

The reason why money makes us greedy is because we want it so much. And the reason why money can keep us away from God is because we're afraid we're going to lose it. Jesus addressed this incredible human tendency toward blatant stupidity (if rejecting eternal life with God for the temporary pleasures of money isn't stupidity, we don't know what is) when He said, "How do you benefit if you gain the whole world but lose or forfeit your own soul in the process?" (Luke 9:25 NLT). Good question. So why do we do what we do when it comes to money? Why do we work so hard to get it and then work even harder to keep it?

We think it has something to do with *ownership*. If there's one quality we humans value above all others, it's self-reliance. And there's nothing that demonstrates self-reliance more than ownership. We love to own stuff because we love the feeling of controlling the details of our lives. It doesn't matter if you're running a multinational corporation or cashing your checks at Paychecks Plus each week; you love the feeling that money gives you.

There's only one way to release money's grip on our lives, and that's to give up the idea of ownership. We've got to realize that God is the real owner of everything we have. No, He doesn't need all your stuff (hey, *you* don't even need all your stuff), but He does want your heart. He wants you to let Him into the details of your life—especially all your stuff—so He can lift you to a higher level of living. "After all," wrote the apostle Paul, "we didn't bring anything with us when we came into the world, and we certainly cannot carry anything with us when we die" (1 Timothy 6:7 NLT).

At best, our job is to manage what God has blessed us with. In fact, that's why God put us on this planet in the first place—to manage *His* stuff, which includes His rivers, seas, plants, animals, and resources.

Don't get us wrong. God doesn't want you to be foolish with His money. Live wisely and share with those in need.

Above all, seek God and His Kingdom first, and He'll provide for everything you need.

- Manage your money as if it belongs to God (because it does).
- There is little benefit to acquiring wealth if you fail at managing it.
- Let money be your servant, not your master.

The generous prosper and are satisfied;
those who refresh others will
themselves be refreshed.
PROVERBS 11:25 NLT

= 18 =

A GENEROUS SPIRIT WORKS WONDERS

The greatest cure for greed is generosity. It's also one of the most satisfying feelings in the world. We're not talking about giving your old clothes to the Salvation Army. (The only thing you'll probably feel by doing that is the satisfaction of cleaning out your closet.) The only way to feel the satisfaction of true generosity is to give away something you value.

This takes generosity beyond money to a realm that includes both possessions and time. That's what the apostle Paul meant when he wrote that we should "be rich in good works and should give generously to those in need, always being ready to share with others whatever God has given [us]" (1 Timothy 6:18 NLT).

The spirit of generosity has become rather stylish in

recent years, and that's probably a good thing. The danger in popularizing generosity is that some people may want to publicize their giving. When that happens, you have to wonder about the true motive. There's also the issue of giving out of your abundance as opposed to giving sacrificially. Both kinds of giving can be useful, but only one gets God's attention.

When it comes to generosity, ask yourself two questions. First, does your generosity come from your heart? A truly generous person gives out of love and compassion, not from a desire to impress others. You also want to give cheerfully, not grumpily. Generosity is incompatible with criticism, resentment, or regret.

Here's another question to ask. Is your generosity productive? In other words, are you giving money, stuff, or time away without accepting responsibility for the consequences? Don't be foolish. Pay attention to the details of where your giving is going. Remember, each time you give to those "in need," you are making an investment of God's resources. Invest wisely. Be a good money manager by making sure your generosity is productive.

. . .IN THE SMALL STUFF

- Money is like fertilizer: it's not much good unless it's spread around.

- Generosity does not include giving away something you'll never miss.

- The generous person always has more than enough; the greedy person never has enough.

We were filled with laughter, and we sang for joy.
PSALM 126:2 NLT

= 19 =

LAUGH AND THE WORLD LAUGHS WITH YOU

You've heard it said that laughter is the best medicine. Well, it may not be the *best* prescription for what ails you, but it is beneficial for your health. Medical researchers have determined that laughter has a profound and instantaneous effect on virtually every important organ in the human body. Best of all, laughter reduces tension as it relaxes the tissues.

At great expense, people join health clubs for cardiovascular exercise. Laughter can produce similar results at far less cost. It stirs up the blood, expands the chest, electrifies the nerves, and clears the brain. Laughter provides refreshment to the entire body.

Abraham Lincoln understood the benefits of laughter when he said, "With the fearful strain that is on me night and day, if I did not laugh I should die."

If you aren't a laugher, become one. Try it. You'll enjoy

it. And if you're having trouble finding something to laugh at, start with yourself. Many people are too impressed with themselves to enjoy their humanity. They are missing out on some great laughs.

Laughing at ourselves gives us a more accurate sense of who we are. It breaks down barriers between others and us. It makes us more approachable. It projects a personality that is warm and friendly instead of rigid and stuffy. Laughter is like a magnet that attracts people. And if you can learn to laugh at yourself, you are guaranteed to have a lifetime of amusement.

Make your home a place that is filled with laughter. That won't be difficult if you look for humor in the small stuff of life. Start with the family photo album. Laughter shared between parents and children is more effective than any curfew. It is a guaranteed formula for producing well-adjusted children. A child who knows how to enjoy laughter is better equipped to handle life as an adult.

Laughter is the secret to a long and enjoyable life. People don't stop laughing because they grow old. They grow old because they stop laughing. He who laughs, lasts.

. . . In the Small Stuff

- The best jokes are painless and profaneless.
- A true sense of humor does not rely on the humiliation of others.
- If you can laugh at yourself, you are guaranteed a lifetime of chuckling.

Don't just pretend that you love others.
Really love them. . . . Love each other
with genuine affection, and take delight
in honoring each other.
Romans 12:9–10 nlt

= 20 =

RELATIONSHIPS TAKE TIME

One hundred years ago, our society was influenced greatly by the farm culture. That lifestyle was slower. There was a season for planting, a season for growing, and a season for harvesting. There was a natural pattern and timetable for living that couldn't be rushed.

Today we live in a technological society where things can't happen fast enough. Everything is instant—from oatmeal to news. Everything is fast—from food to e-mail. We even get frustrated when it takes a few extra milliseconds for the computer to warm up. Our society is characterized by words like: *over-nite*, *drive-thru*, and *on-demand*. We get impatient with anything that takes time.

There is one aspect of life that cannot be rushed—

building a meaningful relationship with another person. You can make an acquaintance "on the spot," but a friendship won't happen instantaneously. And it doesn't develop overnight. It takes *time*. The most precious commodity of our "hurry up" society must be invested over the long term if you expect to have a friendship that is dependable and fulfilling.

Growing a friendship is not unlike growing a crop. There has to be a season of *planting*: time is spent in finding common interests. These initial contacts are followed by a season of *growing*: the friendship is nurtured beyond common interests as you begin to appreciate each other's differences, which are discovered only by spending time together. As the relationship matures, you can begin a lifelong season of *harvest*: this is when the friendship proves to be a source of strength and encouragement to you.

We all want meaningful friendships. We desire relationships that are based on trust and loyalty, those which go beyond shallow courtesy all the way to "do anything for each other" commitments. You can have this kind of friendship, but it will take time. Your time.

. . . In the Small Stuff

- If relationships are difficult for you, then examine your life for the faults you find most irritating in others.
- Commit yourself to projects; dedicate yourself to people.
- Spend more of your time, energy, and resources investing in people than you do investing in things.

A friend is always loyal, and a brother is born
to help in time of need.
PROVERBS 17:17 NLT

= 21 =

YOU NEED YOUR FRIENDS

It's easier to make friends than it is to be a friend. *Making* friends simply involves being nice to people you like. *Being* a friend, on the other hand, involves serious effort. Rather than waiting for others to make you feel better, you make it your goal to add value to their lives. That's why you can't really be a friend to very many people. It's possible to casually and superficially relate to a bunch of acquaintances at one time (kind of like working a room), but being a true friend takes time.

Being a friend is a choice. Here are four different types of friendships you could choose to be involved with. Choosing to establish these friendships will give you great fulfillment, and you will enrich the lives of others.

Be a *disciple*. A disciple is a *learner*. Find someone wiser and more spiritually mature than you are (hint: that person is probably older) so you can *learn* from him or her. Ask this person, also known as a mentor, to meet with you on a regular basis. You may want to do a Bible study together, or you may just want to talk about life.

Be a *mentor*. Even while you are being discipled, be available to teach someone else. Here's where you'll need to be patient, because a mentor doesn't usually seek out disciples. However, if you've got something to offer others and you have the time to be a friend, people will seek you out.

Be *accountable*. In this world of shifting values and vivid temptations, you need to be in an accountability group (this is especially true for men). As a group, discipline yourself to meet on a regular basis (at least once a month) to ask each other the tough questions and to discuss the tough issues.

Be a *neighbor*. When Jesus was asked to name the greatest commandment, without hesitation He replied, "Love the Lord your God," and then quickly added a second commandment: "Love your neighbor as yourself" (Mark 12:30–31 NLT). Loving your neighbor is more than lending tools or cups of sugar. It's care and concern for little things. It's sharing meaningful details from your own life. It's being a friend in such a way that your neighbor will see God in your life.

Friendships are like investments—you get what you put into them, and they take time to mature. But the dividends they pay are eternal.

- A friend is one whose strengths complement your weaknesses.

- Your best friends will criticize you privately and encourage you publicly.

- Make a list of six people you could count on to carry your casket at your funeral. If you can't come up with six, develop some new friendships, or plan to be cremated.

*Don't brag about tomorrow, since you don't
know what the day will bring.*
<small>PROVERBS 27:1 NLT</small>

= 22 =

CARPE DIEM: SEIZE THE DAY

There's nothing we would enjoy more than to sit down together—just the three of us—and talk about how God works in all of our lives every day. The stories we could tell! How God's plan for each of us is unique, drawing upon our strengths and interests, yet similar because we all live for one purpose: to get to know God better.

Of course, we'd love to read about how you're getting to know God—and yourself—better each day (just send your story to our e-mail address). As for us, well, we'd like to leave you with this simple yet powerful challenge: *Carpe Diem*. It means "seize the day."

To quote an old but effective phrase, "Today is the first day of the rest of your life." You can't do a thing to change yesterday, and only God knows for sure what is going to happen tomorrow. So today is the only day you have.

How do you seize the day? First, build upon the knowledge you have that God has worked in your life in the past. Since God "never changes or casts shifting shadows" (James 1:17 NLT) you can have confidence that He will continue to work in every detail of your life. Second, have faith that God has secured your future—no matter what happens. He has given you hope.

If you live in the context of these dynamic beliefs, then you will live in God's power today. When you know that God works through your circumstances, they will energize you.

So go out and make a difference in your world. Leave an impression on everything and everyone you touch because of what God has done for you.

. . . In the Small Stuff

- Live life on purpose, not by accident.
- Surround yourself with friends you have made based on their character, not their compliments.
- Enjoy each day as if it were your last.

> *"For I know the plans I have for you," says the LORD. "They are plans for good and not for disaster, to give you a future and a hope. In those days when you pray, I will listen. If you look for me in earnest, you will find me when you seek me. I will be found by you," says the LORD.*
> JEREMIAH 29:11–14 NLT

= 23 =

GOD IS IN THE SMALL STUFF

We easily find God in nature: the majesty of a rainbow after the thunderstorm; the incredible intricacy of a colony of ants; the still quiet of a moonlit night; or the deafening roar of the mighty Niagara Falls. God is there, and we marvel at His handiwork.

We quickly identify God's involvement in the big celebrations of our lives: the birth of a child; the new job that remedies a financial crisis; or the car crash that left the vehicle totaled but our children unscathed. God is there, and we thank Him for His provision.

And we even acknowledge God's presence in the midst of tragedy: the report from the pathology lab; the severance notice; or the heartache in a home filled with broken relationships. God is there, and we depend upon Him for strength.

Seeing God in these "big things" of life is easy. The more difficult task—yet a challenge just as rewarding—is seeing God in our everyday, mundane activities. We need to have a "God consciousness" about our daily routine. We need a "divine perspective" about the details of life. We must not overlook God in the small stuff.

When we realize that God is in the ordinary, our daily grind suddenly has meaning and purpose. The household chores, whether the lawn or the laundry, become opportunities to express love and care for the other members of the household. A walk to the mailbox brings a chance to greet the neighbor (who may be in desperate need of an encouraging word). The day at work presents the challenge of giving wholehearted effort that will be pleasing to God.

Before He created the universe ages ago, God knew all about us. We should not be surprised that He has ordered our days and is interactively involved in the events of our daily routine. Nothing escapes His notice. Nothing is too insignificant for His care. If we are involved with anything, so is He.

Live your life with an overwhelming sense that God is present in the details all around you. There will be no boring moments. Life will take on new meaning when you begin to see God in the small stuff.

- What happens in you is more important than what happens to you.

- As you go through the day, look for opportunities too good to miss.

- When you see God in the small stuff, your life becomes more meaningful.

—from—

God Is in the Small Stuff
for Your Marriage

It only takes a moment each day
to secure love for a lifetime
BRUCE & STAN

= 24 =

LOVE AND MARRIAGE

There is an old joke about a husband and wife who visit a marriage counselor on their twenty-fifth wedding anniversary. When asked the reason for their visit, the wife complains: "In twenty-five years of marriage, my husband has never said 'I love you' to me." The husband retorts: "I said 'I love you' at the wedding ceremony, and that stays in effect until I revoke it." This joke evokes some laughter from husbands and wives, but it is mostly nervous laughter (because there is a lot of painful truth in this little joke).

One of the quickest ways to choke the romance out of marriage is to take each other for granted. Don't let that happen. Keep the romance in your marriage alive by letting your spouse know that you are so much in love that you can't stop thinking about him or her. Find ways to remind your spouse that he or she occupies your thoughts even though your schedules keep you separated most of the day.

During the phases of dating, courtship, and engagement, you and your spouse probably spent most of your day thinking about each other. And you probably let each other know it, too. Phone calls, e-mails, and endless conversations were evidence that you were always thinking of each other. But with marriage comes familiarity, and while familiarity doesn't always breed contempt (with apologies to Ben Franklin or whoever made that famous quote), familiarity does often bring routine. And in the routine of life we often forget to let our spouse know that he or she remains a priority in our lives—and in our thoughts throughout the day.

Take a lesson from God Himself. He knew human nature. And He knew that Moses and the Israelites could quickly forget about God in the midst of their daily routines even though He had rescued them from slavery in Egypt. (Your spouse forgetting your anniversary seems fairly innocuous compared to the Israelites forgetting that God saved them from the plagues of boils, locusts, frogs, and death that He wreaked on Pharaoh.) God gave specific instructions to Moses to ensure that the Israelites kept thinking about Him throughout the day:

> *And you must love the LORD your God with all your heart, all your soul, and all your strength. And you must commit yourselves wholeheartedly to these commands I am giving you today. Repeat them*

again and again to your children. Talk about them when you are at home and when you are away on a journey, when you are lying down and when you are getting up again. Tie them to your hands as a reminder, and wear them on your forehead. Write them on the doorposts of your house and on your gates.

DEUTERONOMY 6:5–9 NLT

With these kinds of constant reminders, God would not be forgotten or ignored in the routine of the day. Instead, He became a part of the routine.

Your spouse should be an integral part of your day. We aren't suggesting that you put your spouse in first place in the priorities of your life. That place belongs to God. But your spouse should be in second place. And you should take extra effort to make sure that your spouse knows that you are thinking of him or her throughout the day. It shouldn't overload your creativity circuitry to come up with a few ways to communicate this fact. How about going back to those calls, notes, and conversations that you used in the past? Place a "thinking of you" note in a desk drawer, on the car dashboard, or in a text message. Or make a call during the afternoon for no other reason than to say, "I love you."

Don't let the routine of daily living suppress your expressions of love for your spouse. Instead, make sure that your spouse knows that he or she has a place of priority in your thoughts throughout the day.

- Your spouse shouldn't have to think back to your wedding ceremony to remember the last time you said, "I love you."

- You have a lot of things on your mind. Make sure your spouse knows that he or she is one of them.

- Replace the coffee break with a call to your spouse. Instead of caffeine, let romance be your central nervous system's stimulant.

If couples would put half the effort into
marriage that they put into courtship,
they would be surprised how things
would brighten up.
Billy Graham

=25=

DATING DOESN'T STOP WITH THE WEDDING

Remember that combination of nervousness and excitement you felt when you first started dating your spouse? Of course, he or she wasn't your spouse then. The first time you went out, you hardly knew each other. But isn't that why you dated? You wanted to get to know him. You wanted to find out what she was like—and what she liked.

Your dates were fun. You looked forward to a special evening or day, a time you both had set aside so you could spend time together and enjoy each other's company. Eventually, your dating experience convinced you that this was the person you wanted to live with the rest of your life. Then you got married. And the dating stopped.

What a shame.

If dating was so much fun and gave you the opportunity to really get to know your future spouse, why did you stop? Now that you're married, are you no longer interested in having fun? Do you know everything about your spouse that you could ever need or want to know?

Maybe you are at the point where being married is more work than fun. You may be bored with your spouse, and you're looking for some excitement. Look no further. Your spouse still has those qualities that attracted you in the first place, and now there's even more. That's right, whether you realize it or not, your marriage partner has grown in positive ways that you have yet to uncover. All you have to do is make a decision to start dating again, and you will find the wonderful person you married is better and more interesting than ever.

By its very definition, a date is "an appointment to engage in some sort of social activity." So treat it that way. When you were wooing your honey, you didn't just show up on her doorstep unannounced and say, "I'm here, let's go out." You didn't tell your knight in shining armor, "I don't feel like going out. I have a headache."

No, you planned ahead, you came up with a creative idea for your date, you called her up and asked her out. You eagerly anticipated the date, put it on your calendar, and counted the days.

Do the same thing now. Think of a special activity or place, call her up (or call him up), and make a date. As busy as you both are, you need to make an appointment. Then, when the time for the date arrives, get ready. Just like you made yourself look and smell as good as you could when you were dating, look and smell good for your spouse now. One of the keys to a healthy marriage is continuing to attract your husband or wife.

When you are actually on the date, show interest in the other person. Ask questions. You don't know everything about your mate—and besides, he's growing in ways you haven't noticed. She's changing as a person, and you haven't taken the time to discover how. Dating will do wonders for your marriage. It may even revive your relationship.

. . .IN THE SMALL STUFF

- Make dating a habit. Do it once a month at the very least.
- Be creative on your dates, and don't think you have to spend a lot of money.
- It doesn't matter how long you've been married. Always treat your date with respect.

Marriage is the alliance of two people,
one of whom never remembers birthdays
and the other never forgets them.
OGDEN NASH

= 26 =

FINDING OCCASIONS TO CELEBRATE

A celebration can take many forms. It can be a party with family and friends to honor a birthday. A celebration can be rather formal, like a program to commemorate a notable achievement. Or it can be a quiet dinner in your favorite restaurant to celebrate your anniversary.

Like everything else in your marriage, successful celebrations take planning and work. They don't just happen. On the other hand, the important events you intend to celebrate (like birthdays and anniversaries) tend to happen whether you're ready or not. They occur even when you can't remember them, which usually leads to great embarrassment.

Here's our remedy for remembering key events in your married life that happen regularly: put them in whatever calendar you use; and if it is of the digital variety, set up alerts so that you are reminded with increasing frequency as each important anniversary and birthday date approaches. That way you'll have the time to make those dinner or hotel reservations at really nice places, rather than settling for last-minute choices like Burger King or the Motel 6 on the interstate.

Birthdays and anniversaries may be the most obvious reasons to celebrate, but they are not the only ones. We strongly recommend that you find other occasions to celebrate each other and your marriage. In fact, we'd like to go as far as to suggest that you find at least one occasion each month.

A monthly schedule of celebrations coincides nicely with our recommendation to date your spouse once a month. (It's okay to combine your celebrations with your dates, unless you're planning to celebrate with forty other people.) It also shows tremendous respect for your husband or wife and your marriage.

Here are a few ideas:

- You can celebrate achievement: "Honey, you lost those ten pounds you wanted to lose, you look great, so let's go celebrate by buying you some new clothes."

- You can celebrate a promotion: "I knew you could do it, so I've made reservations at the Mother Lode Bed & Breakfast, which we can easily afford with the raise you're getting."

- You can celebrate an accomplishment: "Both kids are in school, so let's go to lunch on Fridays."

And then there are those built-in times of celebration, such as Valentine's Day, Mother's Day, Father's Day, and Veteran's Day. (Hey, you're veterans. . .marriage veterans.) Yeah, the whole world may be having dinner on Valentine's Day, but this is not the time to be a nonconformist. A box of chocolates and a gift certificate to Pic n' Save is no substitute for a dozen roses and a romantic dinner at Chez Pricey.

Finally, try celebrating your marriage on a day separate from your wedding anniversary. Call it your Marriage Anniversary. Here's what you do. Once a year—say, six months from your wedding anniversary—take stock of your married life. Celebrate the blessings, not the battles; focus on the fun you have, not the frustrations you experience. Talk together over dinner and recognize how God has provided for you in every detail of your marriage. See Him in the small stuff of your blessed union of souls, which goes even deeper than your love, right to your very spirit.

Hey, you never know. If this Marriage Anniversary idea takes hold, maybe we can design some cards for the occasion. If that happens, you will be the first to know!

. . .In the Small Stuff

- Generally speaking, a woman would rather have dinner and talk than go to a game and cheer.
- Generally speaking, men prefer an evening where conversation isn't the main feature.
- Don't get stuck in a rut. Plan a variety of celebrations throughout the year.

What we lack is not time, but heart.
HENRI BOULARD

= 27 =

MAKING TIME FOR YOUR SPOUSE

There really is no such thing as "making" time. Time is already made, already measured out in equal doses to everyone. You can't create any more time than you have.

What you can do is redistribute your time so that you spend less of it on the things that don't matter as much, and more on the things that do. The problem we all face is that time is like water in a river: it flows to the place of least resistance. For you that could be work or television or some kind of recreation. Now, work and television and recreation are fine, but if you don't resist, a lot of your "extra" time will flow there, taking time away from really important stuff, like your marriage.

You see, marriage doesn't cry out for time. It's just there, always a part of you. On the other hand, your work is full of deadlines and projects and meetings that clamor for your time. Television is an escape from reality, and recreation is just so much fun. Yeah, marriage has its rewards, but it takes a lot of work.

Bingo. Because marriage takes work, it takes time—time to talk things out, to really listen to your spouse, to reveal your expectations and share your dreams. So how do you get this extra time? By "damming up" those other areas, which means you set time boundaries around them and direct more time to your marriage. That way the time you spend working, watching, and playing won't flood your marriage.

When you purposefully limit the time you spend doing things outside your marriage—work, for example—you aren't necessarily decreasing your chances of success. In fact, your time discipline may actually help you succeed, because you will make more efficient use of your time.

People will respect you for budgeting your schedule so you have enough time for your marriage. And no one will respect you more than your spouse.

. . .In the Small Stuff

- Sit down with your spouse regularly and compare calendars. Make sure you both are happy with the time you are giving to each other.

- Time flies by, but you can direct the direction it flies.

- When it comes to the river of time, we are all in the same boat.

I wouldn't object to my wife having the last word—if only she'd get to it.
HENNY YOUNGMAN

= 28 =

SPEAKING A LANGUAGE YOUR
SPOUSE UNDERSTANDS

Communication problems are obstacles that many marriages can't hurdle. Both the husband and wife can be considerate and well-meaning, but the best intentions in the world won't help if they are speaking different languages. Imagine a marriage in which the husband only speaks Polish and the wife only speaks Portuguese. Plenty of frustrations are going to be in that marriage (especially since the Polish phrase for "I'm sorry, but I don't understand you" sounds very similar to the Portuguese phrase for "You've got the brains of a refrigerator and the face of a frog").

In his book *The Five Love Languages*, marriage counselor Dr. Gary Chapman says that people tend to show love and feel loved predominately in one of five ways:

1. Acts of Service
2. Giving Gifts
3. Words of Encouragement
4. Quality Time
5. Physical Touch

If you are trying to communicate love to your spouse in a way that comes naturally for you (by giving thoughtful gifts even without an occasion), that might not be noticed by your spouse if he or she senses love in another way (such as verbal expressions of affection and encouragement).

This "language barrier" often creates huge misunderstandings in marriage:

- Wife (who speaks the "quality time" language) is thinking: My husband must not love me anymore. He is never at home spending time with me. He loves his work more than he loves me.

- Meanwhile, back at the office, the husband (who speaks "acts of service" language) is thinking: This job is killing me. I'd really rather be at home with my wife, but I've got to keep working hard because I want her to know how much I love her.

Who is at fault here? We wouldn't want to take sides, so we'll just say that it is either nobody or both of them. But there is a problem that needs to be cleared up. The wife needs to recognize that her husband is communicating his love for her in the way that he knows how, and she needs to appreciate his love from that perspective. And the husband needs to realize that his paycheck isn't all that romantic and cuddly to his wife, so he needs to express his love for her in a way that she will understand better.

Learning to speak a foreign language isn't easy. At first it seems awkward. You aren't sure what to say or how to say it. It sounds funny, and you can get a little embarrassed. But if you are in a foreign country trying to speak the indigenous language, your sincere attempts will be appreciated, even if your pronunciation is abrasive.

The same is true when you are "learning" to speak the love language that your spouse speaks. Because it is different from what is natural for you, it may seem awkward. Maybe you won't be exactly sure what you should say and do. But your spouse will recognize the attempt, and your efforts will be appreciated. And as you spend more time speaking that new language, you'll get better at it.

Find out what love language your spouse is speaking, and become very fluent in it. When you do, you might even discover that your spouse is multilingual and speaks several different love languages. Then you can start learning the other dialects as well.

. . .In the Small Stuff

- When it comes to love, actions speak louder than words—but make sure your spouse knows what your actions are saying.

- Thoughtful intentions don't count for anything unless you follow through on them.

- Sometimes the best way to say "I love you" is to pronounce it: "I'm sorry."

*God stands fast as your rock, steadfast
as your safeguard, sleepless as your watcher,
valiant as your champion.*
CHARLES SPURGEON

= 29 =

LET GOD COME BETWEEN YOU

Some say that nothing should come between a husband and a wife: not kids, not career, not finances, not anything. We disagree, sort of. Nothing should come between a husband and a wife that acts like a wedge to divide them and drive them apart. This could happen with any of the circumstances of married life.

But one thing that can come between a husband and wife can actually bring them closer instead of separating them. This is not a spatial enigma. When God is between you and your spouse, He can do exactly that.

When God is in the middle of a marriage, the husband and wife can be closer to each other because they share a spiritual bond. They are connected to each other through

God. A genuine spiritual connection with God is stronger than any other force on earth. Nothing can separate it. And when you are linked with your spouse through that God-connection, your marriage can withstand the circumstances of life that might make other marriages falter.

God is the only priority of your life that should be higher than your spouse. We don't mean to belittle the importance of your spouse by saying that he or she holds the Number Two position. After all, finishing in second place behind God isn't all that bad. And actually, your spouse shouldn't mind, because you will be a much better marriage partner if you follow God's principles for life.

When you think about it, God would make the perfect spouse. He is loving, forgiving, patient, kind, and thoughtful.

Obviously, your spouse falls far short of that standard, and so do you. But you both have a chance of becoming more like that if both of you put God at the center of your marriage and work at reflecting those divine attributes.

God deserves a place in your marriage, and it is right between the two of you.

. . . In the Small Stuff

- Egos can make your marriage overcrowded, but God won't.

- Your marriage will do much better if you include the One who designed it.

- God should be what you have most in common with your spouse.

Successful marriage is always a triangle:
a man, a woman, and God.
Cecil Myers

= 30 =

READING THE MARRIAGE MANUAL

The strength of your marriage will increase as you have more in common with your spouse. But what you share in common must be more than just a favorite flavor of cheesecake or matching "his and hers" pajamas. Oh sure, those things are great if you are splitting a dessert at a restaurant or posing by the fireplace for the Christmas card picture, but they won't do much good at getting you through the tough times in life.

Strong marriages are those where the wife and husband share a similar faith and have consistent values and philosophies. You didn't start out this way as a couple. While you may have had some similarities in your upbringing and backgrounds, you each came into your marriage with your own distinctive sets of beliefs and opinions. Your actions (and reactions) were the product of your life experience before your marriage. During marriage, however, you can work at refining your individual perspectives in the context of what the two of you believe as a couple.

We aren't saying that you and your spouse should each abandon your personal opinions for a kind of generic mental marital mush. But together you should be building a set of values and beliefs that characterize and define your marriage. The Bible is a great place to start the process.

Imagine what the checkout line would be like if your bookstore announced the publication and sale of an ancient book of wisdom that contained the secrets for a successful life. In fact, the Bible is that ancient tome, and every year more copies are sold of the Bible than any other book. While it is worthwhile reading for you or your spouse individually, consider how your marriage could be strengthened as you both read about God's principles for:

- loving marriage relationships
- raising children
- financial matters
- dealing with friends and strangers
- character development
- spiritual growth

Sometimes when couples start to read the Bible together, they feel a sense of awkwardness. The Bible seems a little old-fashioned in our high-tech society. (If that is what's bothering you, then find the scripture online, and read it together on your computer or mobile phone.) But you do a lot of things together and discuss them afterward, such as analyzing the movie when you are driving home. Reading the Bible doesn't have to be any different. Read a passage from the Bible and then talk about it with each other. If you are having trouble getting started, then use a devotional guide that includes an explanation of the passage.

The frequency of reading the Bible together is not as important as establishing the habit. Whether it is once a day at bedtime or once a week on Saturday morning doesn't matter (although you won't get into an actual habit if it is only once a year on Groundhog Day). And the habit is not for the sake of simply creating a ritual or tradition in your marriage. (You could have a tradition of taking out the garbage can together, but it doesn't seem all that worthwhile.) The purpose of reading the Bible with your spouse is to discover, together, spiritual principles that will strengthen both your relationship with God and your relationship with each other.

. . .In the Small Stuff

- The wife and husband who have a Bible that is falling apart probably have a marriage that isn't.

- Other marriage books can give you information, but go to the Bible if you are interested in transformation.

- The Bible can take your marriage from where it is and help you get it where it needs to go.

Marriages are made in heaven.
So are thunderstorms and hurricanes.
AUTHOR UNKNOWN

= 31 =

GOD KNOWS WHAT YOUR MARRIAGE NEEDS

Whom can you go to when you are having problems in your marriage? A friend, a relative, or maybe a marriage counselor? These outsiders may be of some limited help, but their analyses will be shallow. They haven't had the opportunity to know what is really going on in your home.

God is the best marriage counselor you will ever find. Look at what He has to offer:

- He has known both you and your spouse since birth. He knows your personalities. He knows your quirks.

- He has knowledge of what has been happening in your marriage since the two of you exchanged rings at the wedding ceremony.

- He is available to you at your convenience. You won't have trouble making an appointment.

- He doesn't charge $225 an hour.

- You don't have to go to His office. You can use your own couch.

God knows exactly what your marriage needs. And He'll be glad to tell you if you talk to Him about it. Don't expect to hear a booming voice from heaven. God will most likely speak to you through the Bible, in the quietness of your thoughts. And don't expect that God will find that all of the problems are your spouse's fault. He may want you to make some changes.

God wants your marriage to be a success, and He knows how to make it that way. Listen to what He has to say.

. . .In the Small Stuff

- If you're having problems in your marriage, stop complaining and start praying.

- God handles the eternal plans of the universe, so you should be able to trust Him with the problems of your marriage.

- Pray for your spouse—but be ready for God to start changing you.

My definition of marriage. . .it resembles a
pair of shears, so joined that they cannot be
separated; often moving in opposite directions,
yet always punishing anyone who
comes between them.
Sydney Smith

= 32 =

OPPOSITES ATTRACT

Marriages are the combination of two people with strengths and weaknesses that usually offset each other. The wife will have some strong points, and with those she can compensate for the weaknesses of her husband. And the husband will excel in some areas that are difficult for his wife.

If the strengths of each spouse in your marriage counterbalance the limitations of the other, you've got a strong combination. Together you'll be able to manage life's circumstances, because one or the other of you will step up to the plate, depending upon which of you is best suited to handle the situation. This teamwork will give you confidence in your marriage, as well as admiration for the strengths of your spouse.

This teamwork concept in marriage works great, but you shouldn't adhere strictly to it. If you each only do what you are good at, you'll end up being two people who are each operating at 50 percent capacity:

- Don't rely so heavily on the strengths of your spouse that you stop working to improve those areas in which you are weak.

- Don't take on every situation that falls within the areas of your strengths. Leave some for your spouse.

Strengths are good, and you each need to have them. But weaknesses are good, too, because they give you an opportunity for self-improvement. Instead of two people each operating at 50 percent, your marriage can be comprised of two people each functioning at 75 percent. And a marriage operating at 150 percent proficiency will be a real success.

. . .In the Small Stuff

- Keep falling in love with your spouse's strengths, and keep forgetting the faults.

- If you can live with your own flaws, then you can certainly tolerate those of your spouse.

- At the wedding you say, "I do." After that, you should be saying, "We will."

*There is a time for everything,
a season for every activity under heaven.*
ECCLESIASTES 3:1 NLT

= 33 =

SEASONS OF MARRIAGE

Just as there are seasons in nature, there are seasons in life. Even your marriage is not exempt from this principle. As you progress in your married life, both you and your spouse will go through seasons of change and growth (those are the fun seasons). You will also have seasons of dormancy and death—not fun at all, but a necessary part of life.

Here's our take on the seasons of life. As you ponder these, keep in mind that sometimes you will experience them as a married couple, and sometimes as individuals.

SPRING

This is the season of joy, when new growth occurs. Your marriage starts in this season. Your children are born in this season. This is when God seems very close in both the big and small stuff of your marriage.

SUMMER

Ah, those lazy, crazy days of summer. This season is made for relaxing, vacationing, and renewing. This is when your marriage seems like it's in cruise control with no concerns or worries.

FALL

Summer can lull you into complacency. You may even begin to take your marriage for granted. But gradually, some of the things you've worked so hard to achieve start turning sour. Fall is the season of disappointments and unfulfilled expectations. This is the time when you need to take stock of your relationship. Make corrections when necessary and give thanks for the good things you have.

WINTER

Doubt, disasters, disease, and death characterize this season. Nobody willingly enters this time of life, but it will come at different times in your married life. This is the time when God will seem far away and you will feel all alone. That's precisely why you need to call on Him for help and comfort. Make no mistake about it, God will answer—not by removing your winter, but by giving you the strength to get through it.

You may be taken by surprise when a brand-new spring melts your coldest winter. But it will. Just like nature needs every season to continue its course and produce its bounty, you need to go through every season in order for your marriage to thrive.

- Unlike the seasons in nature, the seasons of your life are not predictable.

- The seasons of your life don't come in equal time periods, but they all have equal value.

- God doesn't cause your seasons of doubt and disappointment, but He promises to get you through them.

*You've got to be careful if you don't
know where you're going, 'cause you
might not get there.*
Yogi Berra

= 34 =

THE JOY OF BECOMING

A traditional part of many weddings is the lighting of the unity candle. Three candles are set in a row, with the two outside candles burning (representing the bride and groom before marriage). In a symbolic gesture to represent their new union, the bride and groom each take their respective candle, and together they light the center candle. Then they blow out the flames on their personal candles, and only the center candle remains lit. It is a nice demonstration of the biblical principle that "the two shall become one."

But the symbolism of this unity candle hoopla should not be taken to its extreme. Your own personal life and identity are not snuffed out the moment you become married. You do not lose your individuality, and you are not relegated from a whole person to just half of a couple.

Marriage brings a new dimension of togetherness into your life, but it should not stifle your personal distinctiveness. As an individual, you must still develop and improve yourself. (The same is true of your spouse, but for right now we are just talking about you.)

Don't let marriage stop your growth as a person. Apart from your spouse, you need to continue to improve spiritually, mentally, socially, and physically. Continue your education; get in the habit of reading; pursue a hobby that interests you; develop new friendships; and maintain that exercise program (or at least get one started). It will be great if your spouse can join you in some of these activities, but assume responsibility for your own development.

You don't stop being a person when you become married, so don't stop developing your mind and body. Enjoy the journey of becoming a little better each day. You'll be a good role model for your children (and you might even be setting a challenge for your spouse to keep up with you).

. . .In the Small Stuff

- Make your marriage better by improving yourself.

- Work on changing your shortcomings even if your spouse overlooks them.

- Your marriage began with the two of you becoming one. Don't spend the rest of your lives trying to figure out which one.

Before I got married, I had six theories
about bringing up children;
now I have six children and no theories.
LORD ROCHESTER

= 35 =

WHEN AND HOW MANY

Hopefully, the subject of children will be discussed between the two of you before the minister says, "I now pronounce you husband and wife." It is important to have previously reached an opinion on this issue because:

- Some aunt at the wedding reception will be asking about it.

- Before you return home from the honeymoon, your mother will be knitting little booties.

- You'll freak out when you're shopping for your first home if your choice is a two-bedroom cottage but your spouse insists on an abandoned army barracks (because "we could never fit our twelve kids in two bedrooms").

These issues of "when" and "how many" are very personal for each couple. We won't meddle in your marriage by suggesting a number or a timetable, but we've got a few guidelines:

- Discuss the subject of children with your spouse before you crank up the baby-manufacturing mechanisms. The two of you may have completely different perspectives (especially if you were an only child, and your spouse came from a family where they named the kids in alphabetical order and stopped when they couldn't think of a "Q" name). Remember to discuss your philosophies on discipline.

- Postpone the final decision of how many children you'll eventually have until after your first one is born. Take it one at a time (with the exception of multiple births, and then take it groups at a time). See how you like being parents before you multiply the experience.

- Don't wait for the "perfect time" to have children. It will never come. You will never be prepared financially. You will never have a perfect schedule. You will never have everything ready.

- Don't feel pressured by anyone. Well, you will be pressured, but don't give in to it. If all of your friends start having babies, you are going to feel ostracized. You'll find that the conversations center on disposable diapers, car seats, and breast pumps (and that's what the dads are talking about); you'll be left out if you're still interested in vacations and the stock market. Don't increase the population of your family just so you won't be left out of conversations. (Take our word for it, anything that could be said about breast pumps is not all that interesting.)

- A baby won't solve the problems of your marriage. If your marriage is already on shaky ground, the addition of a child could be like an earthquake.

Children bring a lot of surprises into a family. You can't plan for the surprises, but you can do a little advance planning.

. . .In the Small Stuff

- Children are like mosquitoes. When they stop making noise, you know they are getting into something.
- An alarm clock is a device for waking up adults who don't have small children.
- You think you know a lot about raising children until you have them.

Teach your children to choose the right path,
and when they are older,
they will remain upon it.
PROVERBS 22:6 NLT

PARENTING 101

Parenting is one of the toughest jobs on the planet. By contrast, rocket science is a piece of cake. Managing a large company with hundreds of employees? A cinch. Running a marathon? No comparison. Being a parent is a lot more demanding. It will tax your brain, push you to the limit of your abilities, and take you to the edge of your physical strength like nothing else. But what a ride!

Parenting is not for the timid, but that shouldn't dissuade you from joining the club. The joys of parenting far outweigh the heartaches (as a parent, you'll have plenty of both), and somehow at the end of the day, even though you are totally exhausted and emotionally spent, you decide it's worth doing again tomorrow.

Successful parents seem to have three things in common:

1. They love their children unconditionally.
2. They take the time to get to know their children individually.
3. They put God at the center of their family ritually.

If you're part of a two-parent household, congratulations. That's becoming an increasingly rare commodity these days. Take advantage of your strength in numbers by sharing the parenting duties. Approach the job like a team approaches the Big Game. Your individual efforts won't count as much as you and your spouse parenting together, in sync. And always show love and respect for each other, whether or not the kids are in the room.

If you are a single parent, or a parent with marriage challenges, don't use the kids as an excuse. Don't force them to "pick sides." For the sake of your kids—and more importantly, for your sake—work out your differences. If God seems distant, invite Him into your family through prayer and Bible study. This may sound like a trite answer to some big problems, but you will be amazed at what a huge difference Bible reading and prayer will make to your family.

- Husbands, the best way to show love to your kids is to love their mother.

- Wives, the best way to show love to your kids is to respect their father.

- In order to effectively guide your children, you have to thoroughly know them.

Children are unpredictable.
You never know what inconsistency
they're going to catch you in next.
FRANKLIN P. JONES

= 37 =

THE CARE AND COACHING OF TEENAGERS

The teenagers in your family need a lot of certain things: food, privacy, acne medication, clothes, Internet and texting time, and more food. And they don't hesitate to proclaim their demands for this stuff. (Except they're usually secretive about requests for the acne medication.) But they will never ask for the thing that they need the most: a consistent, positive role model for marriage.

There are a lot of people who are competing for influence over your teenager's life. Don't think that you are out of the competition just because you are a parent. You should be leading the race. You have the greatest impact of all on your teenager's life, but whether the impact is positive or negative will depend upon how well you do your job.

Teenagers have a knack for spotting hypocrisy. They may not see it as easily in their sports heroes or with the entertainment celebrities, but they can sure spot it in your life and marriage. (It's not your fault. Your teenager just doesn't have the opportunity to see the pro athletes and the celebrities in the kitchen at the end of a hard week.) But you have the opportunity to pass along to your teenager great impressions of marriage (of which there are too few examples in the media) if you consistently show love, courtesy, and kindness to your spouse.

Even if you do a fantastic job of raising your children, don't expect that you'll receive a gold medal from your teenager at the awards ceremony for the Parental Olympics. Children, at least while they are teenagers, do not give that kind of recognition and acknowledgment to their parents. Your award will come later, when your children get married and model their marriages after what they learned from you.

. . .In the Small Stuff

- If you want your children to end up with happy marriages, show them one.

- The reason that teenagers think they know all the answers about love and marriage is because they haven't heard all of the questions.

- The best thing you can do for your teenager is to love your spouse.

Everybody knows how to raise children,
except people who have them.
P. J. O'ROURKE

= 38 =

NO KIDS? KNOW KIDS!

What if your marriage doesn't include children? Is your family of two substandard? Are you outcasts in a society that caters to familial units with the "family package" for everything from amusement park tickets to buckets of fried chicken? Are you doomed to experience less than God's best because you hang only two Christmas stockings from your mantel? Absolutely not!

Your marriage is not incomplete if you have no children, but it will be if you don't know children.

If you are without offspring of your own, then you are in the perfect position to develop a meaningful relationship with children whom you could help. Maybe you could fill a grandparent role for some children who have no grandparents in their family. Or, just in case we offended you by suggesting that you could be in a geriatric category, maybe you could fill the role of the hip older brother or sister for a teenager.

The benefit of your relationship with some children

won't be all one-sided. Sure, the kids will get the advantage of your friendship, but you will benefit, too. A child can bring a fresh perspective into your life. You and your spouse will look at things differently, and you'll have a greater sense of wonder and amazement. (If you don't believe us, just go to an amusement park by yourselves, and then go back with a six-year-old.) The benefits for you will depend upon the age of the children with whom you build a friendship. (Teenagers can give you fashion suggestions so you won't dress like the stiffs on CNN.)

You have the rare opportunity to make a difference in the life of a child without some of the routine and hardships that are associated with parenthood. Don't waste this opportunity. There are some children out there who need you.

. . .In the Small Stuff

- If you've got time, you've got exactly what a child needs.

- People who have a hard time understanding teenagers maybe aren't listening to them.

- You may need to make the footsteps for a child to follow.

Out of ego needs, we put our best foot forward
for the people we care the least about,
and our worst foot forward for the people
who mean the most to us.
LANE ADAMS

= 39 =

YOU MARRIED AN ENTIRE FAMILY

Marriage is still popular because most people have no idea what they're getting into. We have this mistaken notion that marriage is an ideal proposition between two people who are hopelessly in love. We dream our dreams and make our plans based on the assumption that we will build our lives together, completely on our own, a cord of three strands that includes just the two of us and God.

How wonderful that we believe that to be true! If we really knew what was about to happen, we might never enter the bonds of holy matrimony.

The thing is, it is just the two of you and God in your marriage. But outside that cozy little marriage cord of three is a bunch of other cords. . .and scraps of twine, pieces of string, and lots of rope. These are your parents, your in-laws, your brothers and sisters, uncles and aunts, nephews, nieces, and cousins. Marriage would be so much simpler if all you had to worry about was the two of you, and the only one you had to please was God. But that's not the way it is. As soon as you say, "I do," you commit yourself to your husband or wife—and his or her entire family.

If you're lucky, your families will give you room and time before cautiously entering your starry-eyed world. However, if you're like most couples, you'll barely have time to warm up the sheets in your new bed before the in-laws on both sides invade your fortress of solitude.

We're not saying that your extended family is bad—and we're not saying they don't mean well. We're not saying they should mind their own business. . .well, maybe we are, and maybe they should! But the reality is that you have no control over what your families are going to do, so you might as well get together on a plan to deal with these other people you married.

Actually, that's the first step. Realize that you married each other, and you also married into each other's family. Understanding this is half the battle. Second, accept the fact that despite information to the contrary, your families really do mean well. When your husband's mother calls, it's not that she doesn't trust you to take care of her baby like she has all these years. She simply misses her son, and without coming right out and saying it, she wants to know if he misses her, too.

When your wife's sister drops by at the most inappropriate moments, it doesn't mean she's nosy. She's just lonely and needs some contact with her little sis.

And when Uncle Jack stares at your beautiful wife at

the family reunion, don't get upset. It's Uncle Jack, for crying out loud. He stares at the Morton's Salt girl on the grocery store shelf.

If you don't like being surprised by relatives, try some preemptive measures. Call your mother (and while you're at it, call your mother-in-law). Take your sister-in-law out to lunch, and buy Uncle Jack a case of Morton's Salt. Get to know your in-laws, which not only shows them respect for helping to raise and nurture your spouse, but also gives you insights into the person you married. The better you get to know that family, the better you will get to know your husband or wife.

. . .IN THE SMALL STUFF

- It may not take a village to raise a child, but it does take a family.
- Keep in mind that all families think other families are a little strange.
- Remember that you and your spouse are part of someone else's extended family.

Life's most persistent and urgent question is:
what are you doing for others?
MARTIN LUTHER KING JR.

= 40 =

LOVE THY NEIGHBOR

The Bruce & Stan research and polling team (that's us with clipboards) has discovered an interesting fact: married couples have a high incidence of vision loss. Our surveys show that if not properly treated, marriage restricts peripheral vision. Now, if you know anything about anatomy or physiology, you might be tempted to challenge our findings. But we aren't talking about ocular clarity. We are referring to the tendency to focus your time, energy, and resources on yourself rather than others.

Self-centeredness is a malady that can plague anyone. You don't have to be married to be self-absorbed. (Narcissists don't usually wed because they are already in love with themselves.) But marriage often causes people to get so involved in their own lives that they forget about others. It can happen without you even noticing it:

- Before you were married, you only worried about one schedule—yours. If you wanted to make time for charitable activities, you only had to check with yourself.

- With the wedding came the difficulty of synching calendars. You have less available time for others because much of your life is coordinated with your spouse.

- The scheduling problems multiply exponentially as you have children.

- And you'll have less "free time" even when you reach retirement. (With doctor appointments and traveling to Branson and Lawrence Welk Village, you won't even have time to see your grandson's Little League game.)

If you aren't careful, your day can be filled with worthwhile and necessary activities that benefit your household exclusively and help no one else in the larger world.

When Jesus was asked which of the commandments was the most important, He boiled down all of the laws of the Old Testament into two requirements:

> " 'You must love the Lord your God with all your heart, all your soul, and all your mind.' This is the first and greatest commandment. A second is equally important: 'Love your neighbor as yourself.' "
>
> MATTHEW 22:37–39 NLT

Jesus said that loving your neighbor is as important as loving God. That must mean that we need to give it a high priority in our lives—even though our schedules are already crammed with personal activities.

Make sure that a part of your married life includes spending time with people who aren't in your family:

- Talk with the kids in your neighborhood. (Answering the door on Halloween night doesn't count.)
- Get involved with a ministry at your church.
- Volunteer in a community program.
- Send letters to friends that you haven't contacted (since you dropped them off your Christmas card list).

If you can participate in these activities with your spouse, that is great. But if the two of you cannot achieve scheduling compatibility, then you should each go it alone, because in the long run, when you give to others, the blessing returns to you doublefold. But make sure you are each doing something that benefits someone else.

Life will be much more rewarding if you spend some of your valuable time doing something kind for someone else.

. . .IN THE SMALL STUFF

- Forget about random acts of kindness until you have done some intentional ones.
- You can't love your neighbors if you don't even know who they are.
- Charity begins at home, but it ought to get out of the house.

We are frantically trying to earn enough to
buy things we are too busy to enjoy.
FRANK CLARK

= 41 =

FISCAL INTIMACY

You can have a few secrets from your spouse. The acceptable confidential categories include: (a) plans for a surprise birthday party; (b) places for Christmas gifts that haven't been wrapped yet; (c) embarrassing nicknames that you were called in elementary school; and (d) any tattoos that were removed before the wedding.

Notice that there is no category for financial matters. Money matters must definitely be discussed with your spouse. There should be no secrets between you in this area.

If your marriage is going through financial struggles, it is unfair to both of you if only one of you knows about it. Both of you need to be aware of the problem, and you both need to be part of the solution. If only one spouse is aware of the difficulty, then the other spouse might unintentionally increase the problem. Friction and resentment will be the inevitable result (as one spouse scrimps while the other records infomercials so as not to miss the offers for tanning lotion, rotisserie cookers, or the car wax that protects the shine even if volcano lava splashes on the hood).

Does this mean you have to present each other with daily cash receipts for your Starbucks coffee? Of course not (although the expense of a twice daily latté habit may require a bank loan after a few months). Does it mean that both of you have to sign every check? No, because one of you probably hates this task and the other might enjoy paying the bills.

You both don't need to know the exact balance in each account, but you both need to have a general idea of how much money you've got and where it goes (and how much is left).

. . .IN THE SMALL STUFF

- Secrets about money can be expensive. They can cost you your marriage.
- Don't let your financial worth be the way you measure the success of your marriage.
- If you've got a good marriage, you'll never be poor (even if you don't have any money).

*This explains why a man leaves his father
and mother and is joined to his wife,
and the two are united into one.*
GENESIS 2:24 NLT

= 42 =

YOURS, MINE, AND OURS

Most of us put ownership right up there with voting and apple pie. We feel that owning stuff is our inalienable right. Once we own something, no one can take it away from us.

So strong is the emotion of ownership that many people let it muddy up their marriage. We all bring stuff to a relationship, and before we marry, it's only proper to keep track of who owns what (after all, the relationship may not work out, and you want to make sure you can get back your set of U2 CDs). But once you marry, there's no need to keep inventory of your personal belongings.

No longer do you belong to yourself; you have become one with somebody else. So has your stuff. If you continue to think of your belongings as yours alone—whether they include cars, furnishings, or children (remember, you don't own them in the first place)—you will only hinder your growth as a married couple. Ownership doesn't just apply to things. You can own a habit or a certain way of doing something so strongly that you refuse to change or compromise for the good of your marriage.

A powerful spiritual principle is at work here. Before you invited God into your life, ownership was all you had. Your focus was on earthly pleasures and life habits in the here and now. When your relationship with God began, your perspective changed. You became a new person from the inside out. As a child of God, you recognize that everything you have and all that you are belong to God. Life is not about ownership now but stewardship.

Unlike an owner, who claims rights to a piece of property, a steward takes care of someone else's belongings. As a Christian, you are compelled to carefully manage what God has given you—and that includes your marriage. Before you were married, you had yours, and she had hers. There was your stuff and there was his stuff. Now it's yours together, and everything you have belongs to God.

- In your marriage, your goal should not be to protect yourself and your belongings. Instead, you should work to protect your spouse, both physically and emotionally.

- Give up the idea of ownership in your marriage and replace it with the concept of stewardship.

- Even as a couple you can be obsessed with your stuff.

*Time is a very precious gift; so precious that
it's only given to us moment by moment.*
Amelia Barr

= 43 =

TIME, PRESSURE, AND FATIGUE

What would you do if you had all the time in the world? How would you react if you could sleep as long as you wanted, as often as you wanted? You might rejoice and fall on your knees in thanks. You would also pinch yourself to see if you were dreaming.

If you are an average person in a typical marriage with the usual schedule (due to work, family, and other commitments), then your two biggest challenges in life are time pressure and fatigue. Don't just take our word for it. Experts like Dr. James Dobson have been saying it for years. One of the unfortunate by-products of our culture is that people are always strapped for time—and as a result, they are very tired.

Perhaps it's because we are a bunch of overachievers,

caught up in the success syndrome. For as long as we can remember, people have been telling us that we can "have it all." Never mind that they were selling beer, cars, travel, clothing, and military service. The messages keep coming—

- You only live once!
- Go for the gusto!
- Be all that you can be!
- The chance of a lifetime!
- Limited time offer!

—until we buy into the fantasy (even if we don't buy all the products).

So the fantasy becomes our driving force, pushing us to achieve more, earn more, buy more, and be more. And the only way we can even get close to realizing our dreams of success is to work harder and do more.

Perhaps we're oversimplifying the problem, but we hope you get the point. Success has a price. There's no free lunch, and only the strong survive. (There go the clichés again.)

Not for a minute are we suggesting that you fail to do your best and shoot for success. We are not endorsing laziness or inactivity. Rising above the level of mediocrity should be your daily goal. But you must go into every job and project, whether you are being paid or not, with your eyes wide open. The Bible calls this "counting the cost." It means estimating in advance how much will be required of you to complete the task. If you can't finish it while keeping your life in balance, don't even start. Otherwise, you are going to run out of time and gas.

Pace yourself. Life is a marathon, not a sprint. Too many of us attack the race like that silly rabbit rather than the wise tortoise, and we end up paying the price. Yes, life takes energy. But it also takes wisdom to know the difference between the costly success and true success.

Time pressure and fatigue can affect your marriage. You may be overcommitted to activities and programs that have nothing to do with work. As we've said before, you can overcommit to some very worthwhile causes, including your church. Before you do, sit down with your spouse and "count the cost." Go in with your eyes open.

Now, before you do anything else, get a good night's sleep!

. . . IN THE SMALL STUFF

- It's easy to say "yes." Saying "no" is what's tough.
- You may not need eight hours of sleep each night, but you need more than you're getting now.
- If you feel there aren't enough hours in the day, you are doing too much.

I want to skip vacation this year
and get a good rest.
LUCILLE S. HARPER

$= 44 =$

VACATIONS ARE SUPPOSED
TO BE A WASTE OF TIME

Your lives are packed with activities: meetings, appointments, errands, and jobs. Time is too precious to waste. And if you're guilty of carrying that same attitude with you when you go on vacation, then you'll hear yourself saying things like:

- We have to drive 487.3 miles today or we will fall behind schedule.

- We'll have an extra morning for sightseeing if we take the plane that leaves home at 2 a.m.

- I've made a list of the top fifty attractions. With six days of vacation, that's 8.3 sites per day.

- I don't care that it's DaVinci's *Mona Lisa*, you're only allowed to spend forty-seven seconds per painting so we can leave the museum in time to see the Cheese of the World exhibit.

We agree that there is an educational benefit to visiting all of the state capitals (but we don't think you have to see them all in a single two-week summer vacation). But your vacations with your spouse don't all have to be of historic value; a few of them should be of romantic value. There needs to be time when the two of you can "get away from it all" and just waste time together.

Don't mistakenly think that romantic vacations all require expensive air travel and a view of the Eiffel Tower or barefoot strolls on the sands of Tahiti. You can find romance at the bed-and-breakfast inn a few hours away (but we're not talking about the downtown YMCA). If you wait until you save the eigth thousand dollars for a trip to France, you may never get there. A weekend at the lake will benefit your marriage more than a dream vacation to Europe that never happens.

These romantic getaways require that you be committed to relaxing and doing it together:

- Husbands: You might want to relax by playing the championship golf course—but if your wife doesn't golf, don't be surprised if she wants to relax by swinging a five iron at your head (or would a sand wedge be better for cranium bashing?).

- Wives: Even though you enjoy it, your husband is going to find little delight in an afternoon spent in the fashion department at Nordstrom's.

Find something you can both do together that will help you unwind. Whatever it is, it won't be a waste of time if you are with each other.

. . .IN THE SMALL STUFF

- The road to romance often requires getting out of town.
- When you're planning to take a vacation with your spouse, agree to travel light: leave your worries and problems at home.
- A change of scenery will change your outlook.

Love is patient and kind. Love is not
jealous or boastful or proud or rude.
Love does not demand its own way.
1 CORINTHIANS 13:4–5 NLT

=45=

THE TRUE MEANING OF LOVE

Love is not something you do. It's more an expression of who you are. This principle is clearly illustrated by God Himself, who is the epitome of love. In fact, that's what the Bible says: "God is love" (1 John 4:8). God ultimately defines love because love fills every part of His being. Since God is infinite and eternal, so is His love.

The amazing thing is that this infinite God of love has decided to focus His love on us, His created beings. Because God made us in His image (Genesis 1:26), He knows us ultimately and intimately. Nobody knows us better than God does, and His greatest desire is that we know Him in return.

There's only one problem. God is perfect and we're not. A perfect being cannot have communion—that is, exchange thoughts and feelings and have a close spiritual relationship—with imperfect beings. That's why God decided to send His only Son, Jesus Christ, into the world to die for our imperfections (in other words, our sin).

God didn't wait for us to love Him on our own. He sent Jesus to die for us while we were still sinners (Romans 5:8). All we have to do is believe that what God did for us is true and effective, the only way for us to have a relationship with Him forever (John 3:16).

Deep down in our souls we long for what God wants to give us: complete intimacy. Intimacy is the key ingredient of love and very much a part of love's true meaning. We are incapable of that kind of love on our own, but with God's help we can both give and receive this true love.

God has designed marriage as the container for true love. Don't let anyone tell you otherwise. Because marriage is ordained by God, it is His sacred gift to us. Marriage is the place where a man and a woman can truly know and truly love each other with every dimension and fiber of their beings—emotionally, physically, mentally, and spiritually.

True love isn't easy, and it doesn't happen by itself. It takes two people trusting God as they work toward the same goal: intimacy.

. . .In the Small Stuff

- There is no way to find true love apart from God.
- God loves you even if you don't love Him.
- The world doesn't need love. The world needs to love.

*The development of a really good marriage is
not a natural process. It's an achievement.*
DAVID AND VERA MACE

=46=

YOUR MARRIAGE IS YOUR GREATEST LEGACY

There's a huge misconception out there about marriage. Many people think that they are the ones responsible for making their marriages work. They have come to believe that somehow in our cleverness, we humans came up with the idea of marriage in the first place. Consequently, the individuals involved are more important than the marriage.

Our society has reduced marriage to a legal contract. In some places all you have to do to get married is make a small payment. This is what happens when we imperfect mortals take something sacred—like marriage—and bring it down to our level. We goof it up! The proof is found in the fact that nearly half of all marriages end in divorce. To avoid this nasty prospect, many couples ignore marriage altogether and simply live together.

If you're married or considering marriage, you need to understand that marriage is more than a contract. Marriage is God's beautiful gift to you and your spouse. It is His idea for you to grow together for life as you both grow in Him. In that respect marriage can be and should be your greatest legacy.

A legacy is something of value you leave to those who follow you. If your marriage is characterized by true love, integrity, and selflessness, then you are telling those around you—especially your children—that marriage is God's idea and not yours. You are saying that your commitment to each other is based on God's standard, not the world's.

As a legacy, your marriage is much bigger than the two of you. It is a representation of God Himself. You see, for people who see God as a formal ritual or an impersonal force, your marriage may be the clearest picture of God's true love they ever see.

. . .In the Small Stuff

- Just because you have trouble doesn't mean your marriage isn't working.
- Your marriage is a greater testimony of God's love and grace than your words.
- The legacy of your marriage will live for generations.

—from—

God Is in the Small Stuff
for Your Family

For you have heard my vows, O God;
you have given me the heritage
of those who fear your name.
PSALM 61:5 NIV

= 47 =

HERITAGE

It is getting tougher to pass wealth on to your children. The IRS imposes gift and estate taxes. Your state may have inheritance taxes. And don't forget those pesky probate fees. It is enough to discourage you from dying. But these problems only apply to an *inheritance* you leave to your heirs. You will be better off, and so will your children, if you concentrate on the *heritage* that you will leave behind.

Don't confuse an inheritance with a heritage. Oh sure, they are both left by ancestors to descendants. But the similarity stops there. An *inheritance* is tangible: it consists of assets and property that can be counted and collected. A *heritage*, however, is intangible: it takes the form of the qualities and values that are reflected in the character of a person's life.

When people think about what they will leave to their heirs, they often focus on the inheritance instead of the heritage. What a tragic mistake. Even though it has nothing to do with wealth, a heritage can be far more valuable than an inheritance:

- A family's heritage can provide a sense of stability and tranquility that transcends the fluctuations of the stock market.

- A family's heritage can foster a moral and charitable spirit that can discern how to share an inheritance with those less fortunate.

- A family's heritage can reinforce a sense of priorities that gives meaning to life, whether the inheritance is large or small.

You may work a lifetime to accumulate an inheritance for your children. But all of your effort can be lost in a moment, during your lifetime or theirs, through financial reversals, economic downturns, or poor judgment. You have no guarantee that it will be put to good use, and it may even cause problems and fights among your children.

Instead of finances, make your greatest gift to your children a rich heritage of personal qualities such as integrity, joy, and spiritual sensitivity to God. Devote your time, energy, and creativity to teaching and modeling such qualities to your children. Preserve and promote these qualities within your family. This is the most valuable legacy you can leave to your children (and it is tax-free, too).

- Pity the poor children who receive a large inheritance instead of a rich heritage.
- You have to die to give an inheritance, but you can add to your family's heritage each day that you live.
- You remember your inheritance when you look at the bank book; you remember your heritage when you look at the photo album.

*Without our traditions, we would be
as shaky as a fiddler on the roof.*
Tevye

= 48 =

TRADITIONS

Does your family seem splintered by a hectic schedule? Is the frantic pace at which you live fracturing your family relationships? Are you looking for a way to bring a sense of permanence, stability, and togetherness back to your family? Family traditions may be the solution.

A family tradition doesn't have to be spectacular or logistically complicated. Sometimes the best traditions are the simplest. A family tradition requires only two components to be successful: it must be celebrated regularly, and everyone in the family must make it a priority.

Think back to your own childhood. What do you remember? Was it spending Sunday nights with ice cream sundaes at the dinner table? Maybe it was going out as a family for doughnuts on Saturday mornings. Or for those of you who were more health conscious, it might have been a special family night to celebrate a good report card. Maybe it was a summer vacation at the same old rickety cabin each year. Perhaps it was always decorating the Christmas tree on the first Saturday after Thanksgiving, always watching *It's a Wonderful Life* (even though everyone in the family could recite the dialogue from memory).

We live in a fast-paced society. Our minds are often focused on where we are going next instead of what we are doing now. Quality moments with the family are at risk of being forgotten in the whirlpool of mundane activities. But family traditions extract us, at least momentarily, from our frantic lives. They provide a sense of stability and predictability. Most important, they provide that most precious commodity: *time*. Time to reconnect with each other; time to talk about things important or trivial; time to simply enjoy being with each other.

Your family will go through stages. An effective tradition in one stage may not work in another. Some traditions may survive; others may need to be replaced. Family traditions can't be forced. They usually happen without fanfare. All of a sudden, you'll find your family repeating a familiar pattern. Find those events and moments. Reinforce them. It will take creativity, energy, and commitment to protect your traditions from the competition of the "outside world," but your family is worth it.

- What you do in your family tradition is not as important as the fact that you do it together.

- Family traditions with your children are your legacy to your grandchildren.

- Family traditions communicate values much more effectively than a lecture.

Cheerfully share your home with those who
need a meal or a place to stay.
1 PETER 4:9 NLT

= 49 =

HOSPITALITY

Hospitality is often defined as the display of thoughtfulness to strangers and guests. That is not too difficult. When you invite visitors into your home, whether they are new acquaintances or special friends, everyone in the family seems to be on "good behavior." Kindness and courtesy fill the air.

But having guests over for dinner is only part of hospitality—the easy part. The more challenging aspect of hospitality happens the moment the door shuts when the visitors leave. Now the real test of hospitality begins: can your family treat each other with the same attention and respect that is reserved for special visitors?

Hospitality is so much more than serving tea and cookies in your home to the Ladies Missionary Guild, or offering your backyard for the company barbeque. It involves creating an environment within the home, and a mentality within your family, that treats everyone as a special guest. Your family members certainly deserve as much courtesy as a stranger receives in your home. Yet the natural tendency is to save our good behavior for the people we hardly know, while our family members are subjected to the less desirable aspects of our personality.

True hospitality creates an atmosphere where everyone, family and guests alike, feels special. It makes your home a place where visitors want to return and where your family feels comfortable. It makes your house the place where everyone wants to be. They won't be coming for the food and beverages (although you'd better keep both in ample supply); they will be at your house because it is a place where they feel appreciated.

This hospitality mentality doesn't happen automatically, and it won't become a habit if it is rehearsed only as often as the good china gets used. It has to be an attitude that everyone in the family adopts. It won't be easy. (Seeing each other in your pajamas seems to destroy the "special guest" illusion.) But with each kind gesture and display of courtesy, your home will become more like a place you would want to visit and stay for a while. That is what hospitality is all about.

- The world is full of places to go, but your home should be the place where people want to stay.

- You know you have mastered the art of hospitality when people leave according to schedule with the impression that they could have stayed forever.

- In a hospitable home, everyone serves each other because they all feel special.

*And you must love the LORD your God with all
your heart, all your soul, and all your strength.
And you must commit yourselves wholeheartedly to
these commands I am giving you today. Repeat them
again and again to your children. Talk about them
when you are at home and when you are away
on a journey, when you are lying down
and when you are getting up again.*

DEUTERONOMY 6:5–7 NLT

= 50 =

GOD

What role should God have in your family? Should He be relegated to an insignificant influence, or should He have preeminence over all things? The correct answer is obvious, but sometimes the life we lead suggests that we have gotten our priorities mixed up.

Does your family talk about God in the context of your everyday circumstances? If His name is only mentioned as an expletive, then you should not be surprised if God seems nonexistent.

Does your family turn to God only in times of crisis or emergency? Certainly God is there in those times, but He may seem distant to you because your contact with Him is so sporadic.

Does your family treat God like a holy rabbit's foot. . . looking to Him for good luck and protection? This concept of God might actually lead to a lack of faith in Him when your "luck" turns bad.

Or maybe your family interacts with God only as a religious ritual. It is as if you have Him in a box, and you bring Him out for display on Sundays and major religious holidays. The rest of the time, you keep Him in the box on a shelf in the closet, where He won't interfere with your daily activities. If this is your approach, your family must think of God as cold and impersonal.

God deserves a place in your family, and it is *first* place. And your family deserves to know God is real and personal. They need to know that He is vitally interested in the events of their lives. . .from the major events to the minor circumstances. But God won't intrude on you or your family. He is like a perfect gentleman, waiting to be invited as a guest into your lives.

Your family can experience the real and living God, but you must approach this relationship like others that you value. You can't expect to develop a close friendship with someone whom you totally ignore. You need to acknowledge God's presence, recognize His activity in your lives, and appreciate His provisions. Stated simply: you need to make room for God in your lives. When you do, you'll be amazed at the difference. You'll see God's hand directing you, you'll hear His voice comforting you, and you'll sense His Spirit embracing you. He will be real to you.

Although God deserves to have priority in the lives of your family members, don't do it just for His sake. Put Him in first place for the sake of your family.

. . .IN THE SMALL STUFF

- We should give God the same place in our family that He holds in the universe.

- Let God have control in your family. He can do more with them than you can.

- If you keep God outside of your family, there will be problems inside your family.

He cannot have God for his father who refuses
to have the church for his mother.
SAINT AUGUSTINE

= 51 =

CHURCH

God loves families. After all, He designed the concept. In His plan, family units are the basic building blocks of society. God also used a "family" blueprint when He designed the Church. But while a church may be composed of many individual families, God intends that all of the church members interact together as a single family. The similarities (and benefits) may surprise you.

An obvious similarity is the intergenerational composite of the family and the Church. Just as your extended family may include infants and seniors, the members of the Church span the age spectrum. Think of how this arrangement can benefit you if you regularly participate in a church. Your church family can provide you with the exuberance of the young and the wisdom of the mature.

Within this context of diversity you can appreciate qualities, experiences, and opinions of people with perspectives different from your own.

With a family, there is a sense of belonging. Your family ties give you a sense of identity and a sense of being connected to something larger than yourself. So it is with a church. Under the authority of the heavenly Father, you can enjoy a brother and sister relationship with your "church family." You may be surprised to notice that you can grow as close to the members of your church family as to those in your biological family. In a church operating as God intended, you will have continual support and encouragement. You won't have to endure sickness or misfortune alone; some of your "brothers and sisters" will be by your side. You will want to share all of the events of your life, whether in celebration or sorrow, with your church family. They will be cheering you on in victory, and consoling you in defeat. And you will be doing the same for them. . . because that's what being a family is all about.

A family has a shared heritage, and so does the Church. With the family, you can pull out the family photo album and see the common ancestors—the lineage that connects you. In the Church, you won't have a photo album, but you do have a book that clearly identifies your common ancestry: the Bible. This doesn't mean you can trace your family tree back to Adam and Eve, but your shared belief in the God of the Bible connects you with each other. In this sense, the bonds of the Church may be stronger than those of your biological family. After all, you didn't get to pick your biological ancestors, and you may have little in common with your relatives (at least you'll think so after the family reunion). But with the members of your church family, you are bonded by a common love of God and commitment to the Scripture.

God designed the family to function together in harmony: the husband honors his wife and serves her with sacrificial love like Christ displayed; the wife, in turn, responds with love for her husband; the children love and honor the parents; and the parents raise the children with responsibility and respect. The relationships in the "church family" are to operate the same way. No one is more important than anyone else; everyone has a role in contributing to the spiritual growth and encouragement of each other.

But we can't ignore the obvious. A variety of nuts grow on your family tree, and with some of them you would prefer to saw off their branch. And in your church you'll find a few oddballs, too. But this is no reason to stay away altogether. Remember that if the Church only admitted people who didn't need it, you couldn't attend either. If a few people irritate you, view them as an opportunity to practice the godly virtues of patience and forgiveness *and love*.

Your personal family is not perfect, and your church family won't be either. But all the good aspects God intended for a family can be found in a church. That family is not complete without you, and you aren't complete without them. That's the way God designed it.

- Church is where you will meet family you never knew you had.

- You are never too bad to go to church, and you are never too good to stay away.

- With your relatives, the family resemblance is usually seen in the face. With your church, the family resemblance is usually seen in the heart.

God loves a cheerful giver.
2 Corinthians 9:7 niv

= 52 =

STEWARDSHIP

There is a good barometer for telling how your family feels about God: money. Now, wait! Before you mistake us for those types on television who say God's blessings are in direct proportion to the amount of digits on your contribution check, let us explain. We aren't talking about *how much* you give. (We hear you breathing a sigh of relief.) God is more interested in your *attitude* about giving than the *amount* of your giving. Your attitude about money reveals much about your relationship with God.

"Stewardship" is the way in which you handle what God has given to you. Of course, you want your family to be good stewards of the finances God has given to you. But stewardship means much more than throwing bucks in the offering plate, clipping newspaper coupons, or being a whiz with your Quicken software. While your charitable contributions and responsible budgeting are a part of it, there is much more to stewardship than that.

Stewardship involves perspective. Your family needs to realize that everything you have comes from God. Oh sure, one or more of you actually brings home a paycheck, but God worked in the circumstances that provided the job.

Stewardship involves priorities. When does God get "paid"? Is He the last one? Are you giving to your church and the other ministries only after everything else has been purchased and paid for? Is God getting just the leftovers (if there are any)? God deserves first place in our lives. That means our finances, too. Giving a portion to God first reflects an attitude that God has priority in your family finances.

Stewardship is a privilege. Are you excited about giving to God? You should be. God doesn't really need our money, but our gifts can be an expression of our gratitude for His constant provision. Also, your gifts can be used in ministry to help others. When we understand what God has done for us, we will consider it a privilege to help others.

Your household probably isn't any different from most other families. The paycheck proceeds are in high demand. Everybody wants a chunk, and there may not be enough to go around. But God isn't standing in line with His hand outstretched. He wants you to respond and come to Him on your own. Whether you are willing to put something in His hand reveals what is in your heart.

- What you earn affects the quality of your living; what you give affects the quality of your life.

- If you think you can't give when you have little, then you won't give when you have much.

- If you give generously to God, He won't be any richer, but you will be.

Laughter and weeping are the two
intensest forms of human emotion,
and these profound wells of human
emotion are to be consecrated to God.
OSWALD CHAMBERS

HUMOR

We know that you are willing to do whatever it takes to strengthen your family. Whether it is time or energy or money, nothing would be too great a price if you could be assured that the family relationships would be improved. Well, we can't give you any guarantees, but we do have a suggestion that has a proven track record and a low cost.

We believe that a sense of humor can be a secret formula for success in your family. Laughter softens the rough edges in the relationships between family members. When your family is laughing together, all of the barriers that might separate them seem to disappear.

- The "hard feelings" over a past disagreement dissipate with laughter. Somehow the argument won't seem so important after a few mutual chuckles.

- Parents can't take themselves too seriously when they have a sense of humor about their idiosyncrasies and weaknesses. Your children will appreciate the fact that you are open and honest about your faults. (These flaws are painfully obvious to your children, so you might as well laugh about them. And your children will appreciate the fact that you aren't hypocritical and pretending to be perfect.)

- Your children will have an improved self-image if they can laugh about themselves. They will realize that it is okay to be less than perfect. They will learn to accept and appreciate their own uniqueness. With a healthy attitude about their own peculiarities, they will have a strong defense against peer pressure.

- You don't have to be a stand-up comic to pull this off. All it takes is a lighthearted spirit. A lively attitude. Playful teasing. A few practical jokes. Just make an effort, and you'll find that humor and laughter have a momentum that builds as others join in.

We suppose it is every parent's dream that their children will have fond memories of life at home. It is difficult to predict what memories they will carry with them in the future, but there is a way that you can monitor their impression of how things are going in your home right now. Look at their faces. Do you see grins or grimaces?

- A sense of humor is a sign of sanity.

- Laughter is the best medicine, even if you aren't sick.

- There is no loneliness in a home filled with laughter.

Wherever you go, God is there.

= 5 4 =

TRAVEL

We are big proponents of family travel. Getting out of the house and into a different environment can have many benefits for your family. Together you can experience new adventures. Together you can meet new people and see new sights. In these different situations, the foreign circumstances will bond your family together.

A trip to a foreign country can be a particularly enlightening and cohesive experience for your family. But don't think that you have to postpone family travel until you have saved the price of a new house to stay a week in Paris. Your family travel doesn't have to be that extravagant.

One particular family travel event can be inexpensive—and it is guaranteed to give you the greatest opportunity to create memories and see God's provision all at the same time: the family car trip. An adventure of this sort is not for the faint of heart, but look what awaits you:

- You will learn patience as you answer the repeated plea for the "ETA" (estimated time of arrival—which is the contemporary version of "Are we there yet?").

- You will learn dependence upon God's provision as you find your way after being lost.

- You will learn to trust God for protection as you are changing the flat tire on the shoulder of the interstate.

- And perhaps most important of all, you will be learning these lessons together as a family (if you are bold enough to admit to your kids that you are lost). These are excellent opportunities to teach your children about God being in the middle of your circumstances.

Some of the memories from car trips will last forever. Oh, your kids may forget about the side trip to see the World's Largest Ball of Twine or the Petrified Mushroom Garden, but they will remember laughing at each other's antics, singing together, and playing car games to pass the time. And after all, isn't that what family outings are all about?

So, whether it is a chateau in Southern France or the Motel 6 in Fresno, include family travel on your agenda. Even a weekend journey can be a trip that lasts a lifetime in the memory of your family.

- Sometimes you strengthen your home when all of you get away from it together.

- You have to go away to learn that there is no place like home.

- The family that travels together experiences God together.

To keep your marriage brimming,
With love in the loving cup,
Whenever you're wrong, admit it,
Whenever you're right, shut up.
OGDEN NASH

= 5 5 =

MARRIAGE

Marriage seems to be the favorite topic of comedians. Everyone laughs at the descriptions of a husband who is either snoozing in the recliner, belching and scratching, or driving around lost but refusing to ask for directions. And the stereotypes of the wife aren't much better. She is usually described as a nag, a shopaholic, or a neat freak. But the disrespect of most spouses for each other is no laughing matter. Let's face it. Most married people believe that a spouse is like arthritis: a bit of a pain, but you learn to live with it.

Marriage doesn't have to be that way, because God didn't design it that way. In God's plan, marriage is a lifetime union between a husband and wife, a union that completes each of them. Together they are a whole. They complement each other and bring to the relationship exactly what the other needs.

Instead of laughing at your spouse, or focusing on those habits that irritate you so much, try looking at your spouse from God's perspective. God specifically and uniquely designed your spouse *for you*. The Master Designer knew the kind of person you would need to smooth out your own rough spots. So look for the strengths in your spouse that offset your weaknesses. Instead of tuning out what your spouse says, consider that those words may be exactly what God wants you to hear.

This new perspective won't come easily. After all, you have probably spent most of your marriage (beginning shortly after the honeymoon) trying to change your spouse. It may take some time to reprogram your own thinking to recognize that God may be using your spouse to change *you*.

And there's more, too. Just as God is using your spouse to work in *your* life, you are God's most obvious method of ministering in your *spouse's* life. If God wants your spouse to be comforted or encouraged or consoled, who is He most likely to use for that purpose? You! Quit the ridiculing and complaining that seems to come so naturally. God wouldn't talk to your spouse like that, and He doesn't want you to do so either. Talk to your spouse like God would. (Don't feel obligated to use those fancy "thee's" and "thou's." God doesn't speak in King James English anymore.) Remember that God wants to use you in your marriage to spiritually and emotionally support your spouse.

Think about the transformation that can occur in your

marriage if you both attempt to be God's servant to each other. No longer will your marriage be characterized by vicious sarcasm or ridicule. Instead, each of you will be looking for opportunities to help the other. And if you welcome your spouse's input as being helpful instead of hurtful, you will stop being defensive with each other.

How sad that many marriages are tolerated instead of celebrated. But what else can we expect when the relationship is like a battlefield? By appreciating what God wants to accomplish in your life through your spouse—and by understanding the role you play in God's effort to minister to your spouse—your marriage will become a sanctuary. It will be a place to which you both retreat for mutual protection, care, and comfort. You will feel safe in your marriage because the relationship will be free from character assassination. In a hectic and hostile world, your marriage will be your place of refuge.

Try to see yourself and your spouse from God's perspective. It will change the way you live. It will change the way you love. And that is no laughing matter.

. . . In the Small Stuff

- You can contribute more to your marriage with an open mind than an open mouth.

- Before marriage, you should concentrate on finding the right person. After marriage, you should concentrate on being the right person.

- With the faults and failings of your spouse, have a thick skin and a short memory.

Don't let anyone think less of you
because you are young.
1 Timothy 4:12 NLT

= 56 =

TEENAGERS

The teen years are difficult. For both the kids and the parents. Teenagers are at an awkward stage:

- They aren't yet adults, but they think they are.
- They have outgrown being little kids, but at times they still act like them.
- They want to be independent, but they want their parents to pay for everything.

Part of the difficulty of living with teenagers is their failure to live up to the parents' expectations. You might assume that this is the fault of the teenagers. Well, maybe. But perhaps a share of the blame can be placed on the parents for having *unrealistic* expectations. Now, don't get us wrong. We aren't parent-bashing here. (After all, we have been parents for a lot longer than we were teenagers.) We just know that when you're under the pressure of being a parent, it is easy to forget that teenagers are still behaviorally schizophrenic—sometimes they act like adults and sometimes they don't.

Parents often make the mistake of remembering the fleeting times when their teenager showed responsibility and maturity, and then the parents use that behavior as the standard. But the teenagers won't always measure up to that benchmark because their maturity isn't consistent yet. Teenagers have "transitory maturity." It comes and goes. (Hopefully, over time, the maturity will stay a little longer each time it comes.)

It might be helpful if you discuss your expectations with your teenagers. We suggest expectations that are based on the evolutionary stage your teenager is going through. We don't mean that your teenager is a Neanderthal (although there are times...). We just know that it is unrealistic to expect constant perfection (because parents can't even reach *that* goal). Here are a few examples (and we expect that your teenager will like the odd numbered ones, and you'll appreciate the even numbered ones).

Expectation #1: *Expect your teenagers to make mistakes.* They will be able to live up to this expectation. In fact, they may be overachievers on this one. But if your expectations include mistakes from your teenager, then you won't be surprised when they happen. Oh, you may still get disappointed, but perhaps you won't pop a cranial corpuscle.

Make sure that your teenagers know that Expectation #1 does not entitle them to make mistakes intentionally. It is reserved for mistakes that they make out of ignorance, immaturity, or sheer stupidity. It doesn't cover goofing up on purpose. (See Expectation #2.)

Expectation #2: *Expect your teenagers to learn from their mistakes.* This is an important corollary to Expectation #1, and it recognizes the transition of teenagers from childhood to adulthood. Making honest mistakes is part of being a kid; learning from mistakes is a part of being an adult.

Expectation #3: *Expect that your teenagers won't tell you everything.* As part of the journey to independence, your teenager will want more privacy. (Crawling into the clothes hamper with the cell phone is a clue.) Your curious inquiries will be viewed as cruel interrogations. Learn to be satisfied with monosyllabic responses.

Expectation #4: *Expect that you will be informed about the "who, what, where, and when" away from home.* Expectation #3 is an accommodation to the teenager's desire for privacy. Expectation #4 reflects the parent's duty to protect, teach, and advise their children. (If your teenagers scoff at the need for such supervision, remind them about Expectation #1.) So, given your parental responsibilities, it is reasonable to expect that you will know "where, when, what, and who" whenever your teenager isn't at home.

Expectation #5: *Expect that you won't be your teenager's best friend.* As much as you think that you are "cool" and "with it," your teenager thinks that you are old and outdated. (The fact that we use lingo like "cool" and "with it" proves that we are of a bygone era.) So, your teenager probably won't want to hang out with you at the mall. (And if you have to go there together, don't be surprised if you are ignored. . .or called by your first name instead of "Mom" or "Dad.")

Expectation #6: *Expect to be treated with respect.* Your teenager doesn't have to treat you like a best friend, but you at least deserve to be treated like a fellow human being. Common courtesy should not be abandoned just because you are related.

If these work for your family, please let us know. Unfortunately, we didn't think of them until after our kids had outgrown their teen years. Our children aren't the only ones who are smarter now than they used to be. So are we.

. . .IN THE SMALL STUFF

- Your teenager hasn't had enough time to outgrow all the faults that you used to have.

- Teenagers think that they know all the answers, but they haven't heard all the questions.

- No one is as smart as teenagers think they are, and no one is as dumb as teenagers think their parents are.

"Grandma, do you remember what it is like
to be a little girl like me?"
"Of course, darling."
"Grandma, do you remember what it's like
to get candy for no reason?"

= 5 7 =

GRANDPARENTS AND GRANDCHILDREN

You wouldn't try to sit on a milking stool that only had two legs. That would be foolish (unless you're a lawyer looking to sue the dairy farmer). A two-legged stool has no stability. It needs the third leg for balance and strength.

The same is true for families. No, they don't need a third leg. But they do need a third generation. There needs to be a relationship between grandparents and grandchildren. That third generation brings stability, balance, and strength to the family.

Grandparents bring a sense of history and heritage to the family. They can testify to God's continual provision through the years. Their lives tell the story of how God works in the details and circumstances of day-to-day events. Look for opportunities for your parents to tell their personal stories to your children (and your kids may be particularly interested in hearing tales about your behavior as a child).

With you, your kids will only be children. With your parents around, your kids will have the opportunity to be grandchildren. No child should ever miss the privilege of being a grandchild. Grandchildren get preferred status. A child gets disciplined, but a grandchild gets spoiled. There are rules for a child, but a grandchild has no limits. Grandparents will give your child the opportunity to be loved without demands or expectations. Include grandparents in family activities as often as possible, but also arrange for your children to spend time alone with their grandparents.

Don't despair if death or distance has robbed your family of that "third generation." There are many "grandparents" who are waiting to be adopted. You can find them in your neighborhood or in your church. The adoption process is easy. (It can get started at the dinner table or with a trip to the zoo.)

Grandparents can give your children a sense of acceptance. Grandchildren can do the same thing for your parents. You'll get the benefit from both ends of the generational spectrum.

- Maybe the grandchildren wouldn't get so spoiled if you could spank the grandparents.

- Grandparents make great babysitters. They watch the grandchildren instead of the television.

- Time with grandparents is a vacation from reality.

*Whether or not you enjoy your family reunion
is entirely up to you. It's all relative.*

= 5 8 =

FAMILY REUNIONS

At the appointed time, they begin to arrive. It is a strange assortment of humanity: some appear to have lived under rocks, or traveled with the carnival sideshow, or escaped recently from the penitentiary for the criminally insane. From all directions, they converge on your home. Is this a scene from the latest Stephen King made-for-television thriller? No, it's the family reunion!

Fear grips you as you open the door and begin to greet this bizarre assortment of cousins, and the in-laws of the cousins, and the friends of the children of the. . .hey, who are those kids, anyway? As you watch in helpless terror while your home is soiled and stained, you are comforted by your previous decision to defer recarpeting until after this fiasco. As you see your personal effects being fondled and sat upon, you find solace in your earlier precautionary measures of hiding everything of value that could be broken (or stolen).

Finally, the event is over. Like a frightened squirrel, you huddle on the couch to enjoy the silence of your own thoughts. Although you dare not speak these thoughts audibly, you come to the obvious conclusion that you are the only normal one in the entire family tree. (Unbeknownst to you, everyone else is thinking exactly the same thing about themselves as they leave your home.)

The scene we have just described was exaggerated (sort of). While we may feel some apprehension about family gatherings, they are never as bad as we dread. In fact, such periodic reunions can strengthen your family spiritually and emotionally. You will find that they can be very rewarding if you remember that God invented the family and has put you in one for a reason.

Family reunions also allow you to appreciate the diversity within your family tree. Enjoy the variety of personalities and perspectives. Value each relative for the differences he or she brings to your group.

Although each family member is a distinct and unique person, you shouldn't forget to appreciate the common bonds of ancestry that you share. In a time and society when people are lonely and detached, you will gain a real sense of belonging when your extended family meets together. Through your ancestors you can trace your nationality and ethnic roots. It probably only takes a few generations to trace your heritage to some other continent.

Your spiritual heritage, just like your family heritage, also may be graphically depicted by each life represented in the group. One ancestor may be responsible for bringing a godly influence and sensitivity to your family. If so, you can thank God for that person. Or you may realize that you are the one God has chosen to bring a spiritual influence to your family.

When the family reunion is all over, you might find yourself laughing about Uncle Harold's peculiarities. When the chuckling has subsided, don't forget to thank God for the beautiful, diverse gift of your family lineage.

. . .IN THE SMALL STUFF

- Don't complain about the relatives you are stuck with. Remember that they didn't get to make a choice about you either.

- Distant relatives don't have to stay that way.

- Geographic separation is no excuse for not staying in touch.

For many people the heavy responsibilities of home and family and earning a living absorb all their time and strength. Yet such a home— where love is—may be a light shining in a dark place, a silent witness to the reality and the love of God.
OLIVE WYON

= 59 =

WORKING PARENTS

It's nearly become a fact of family life that both parents work. And if yours is a single-parent household, it's a virtual certainty that Mom or Dad (either of which could be you) works full-time.

Sometimes work can be very fulfilling. Other times it's a necessity and little more. Often it's difficult to balance the pressures of work with the demands of running a household and raising a family. We think, *If I keep this schedule up, something's going to suffer.* But it doesn't have to be that way.

You may not be able to change your working situation,

and we're not saying you should. We're not going to tell you that your family will deteriorate if you work, unless work has become the central focus of your life. What we'd like to suggest is that you keep your work and your family in balance by seeing both as special and sacred callings of God.

The Bible is clear that husbands and wives are to love and respect each other. As parents they are supposed to encourage rather than frustrate their children, who have a responsibility before God to obey their parents (it's all in Ephesians 5 and 6). From what the Bible says, these responsibilities continue as long as you are—(a) married; (b) still have kids around; (c) still have parents around; or (d) any of the above—which is basically your entire life.

Now, you probably knew that. It figures that God wants us to pay attention to the details of our family relationships. But did you know that God also cares about your work? Absolutely. God isn't some old-fashioned, out-of-touch, gray-haired Being who doesn't know what you're all about and what you're going through. He knows everything about you and your relationships, and you can be sure He knows about your work.

He knows that you probably spend half your waking hours in a job, and He knows how important that job is to your livelihood and your self-esteem. Your work matters to God.

That's why the Bible tells us, "Settle down and get to work. Earn your own living. And I say to the rest of you. . . never get tired of doing good" (2 Thessalonians 3:12–13 NLT). Whether you're flipping burgers or writing computer code, you have the opportunity every day to show your boss, your coworkers, and your subordinates just how much God matters to you. And the best way to do that is to work to the best of your ability with the highest integrity every single day.

. . . In the Small Stuff

- Your work family is important, but it should never become more important than your real family.

- Your coworkers should know you're a Christian by your actions more than your words.

- There will be times when the demands of work will overshadow your family. Make sure your family knows this is only temporary.

As he was packing his meager possessions to
move out on his own, the son looked fondly
(and enviously) around his parents' home.
As he gazed at the house, the furniture,
the yard, and the food, he asked,
"Dad, why would I leave all of this?"
His dad quickly replied, "Because
it is not yours!"

LETTING GO

If you have already had a child leave home, you know what we are about to discuss. If it hasn't happened to you yet, get ready. It won't be easy.

God helps prepare parents for this transition by making the kids go through the teenage years. Those can be trying years for a parent. There may be times when you doubt if your teenagers will ever leave home...because you might strangle them first. But as the actual time approaches, whether it is "off to college" or just "moving out on their own," both parent and child get an overwhelming sense that this event marks a transition in their relationship. The change of circumstances brings about an immediate change in the dynamic of the parent/child relationship. From this point forward, your relationship will be drastically different, and there will be no going back.

There will be mixed emotions as you "let go." You will struggle between *what you want* versus *what is best for your child.*

- All of a sudden you will want your child to stay. Your child's irritating habits will suddenly become endearing traits. You will want the dirty laundry piled in the bedroom. You will want the bathroom to be a mess. You will want the refrigerator door left open and the phone line occupied. (Well, maybe. . .)

- But you will know that your child needs to leave. Keeping your child at home is what you want for yourself, but allowing your child to leave home is what you want for your child. And you will know that what you want for your child is more important than what you want for yourself.

You will not be alone with your feelings. God knows exactly how you will feel. He had a Child leave home, too. But God knew in advance everything that would happen to His Child, and you will know nothing about what will occur in the life of your child. So, talk to God about it. You can pray about your child's past and about your child's future.

- For the past, pray that God will give your child a selective memory. You want your child to remember your strengths and forget those times when you disappointed your child (and God). You want your child's recollections to be of "Kodak moments," or at least of memories when you were trying your best for your child's best.

- For the future, pray that God will guide both of you in learning, understanding, and enjoying the evolution of your relationship. Pray that you can move gracefully from rule-maker/enforcer to advice-giver. Pray that your mouth will move only after your ear has listened. Pray that God will change your language from instructions to advice. As for your child, pray that God will instill a realization that you have no greater interest than his or her well-being. Pray that your child will be inclined to ask for advice when necessary. Pray that your child will have the wisdom to know which advice is priceless and which advice is worthless.

No matter how much you have prepared for the day of "letting go," it won't be enough. You will have done a better job at preparing your child than preparing yourself. So don't forget to pray for yourself. Pray that you will have full confidence in God's promise that He can keep your life in *peace* even when it seems to be broken in *pieces*.

Before He formed the universe, God knew the day when your child would be leaving home. He has great plans to work in the life of your child—plans that require you to "let go." You need do your part, so God can finish His part.

- "Letting go" means shifting from instruction to influence.

- Moving out is an essential part of growing up.

- "Letting go" can be a matter of perspective: you aren't losing a child; you're gaining a bathroom.

God is our refuge and strength,
always ready to help in times of trouble.
PSALM 46:1 NLT

= 61 =

CRISIS

No one wants to go through crises, but you can't insulate yourself from them. They often happen unexpectedly. . .and tragically. It might be a severe financial reversal, or sickness, or even death. It may be rebellious children or a fractured marriage.

You may have no control over the events that trigger the crises in your family, but you have the choice of how you are going to respond. The manner in which you react to the crises could make matters better or worse. In the midst of calamity, you might not be thinking objectively. So now, in this quiet moment, let's consider how God could use a crisis for good in your family.

Tragedy could potentially splinter a family, but it could also be the basis for bringing family members together.

Adversity can be endured more easily with friends and family by your side. Lasting bonds of love and friendship can be forged through tough times because you "were there" for each other. Many people often shy away from family and friends in the midst of catastrophe because they don't know what to say. But the words aren't important. Your presence is all that may be required; your availability will speak from your heart the words that your mouth cannot say.

Just as difficult times can unite you with your family, a crisis may be the event that reconnects you with God. He often gets forgotten in the "good times" when you are thinking that you are self-sufficient. (While you might never say so, your actions might indicate that you think you have no need of God.) But when the money runs out, or your health is in jeopardy, or the children are in trouble, you can turn to God and He will be there. No appointment necessary. You don't have to take a number. And you won't get stuck with His voice mail. You can speak directly to Him, and He can make Himself known to you.

The tough times you endure can also be a way to prepare and equip your children to handle difficulties in their future. You wouldn't want your children to succumb to their problems with whining and self-pity, so don't let them catch you responding to your troubles that way. Your perseverance in the face of adversity is a lesson your children need to learn, and you can be the best teacher.

The devastation of any crisis will be minimized if you use it as an opportunity to bring your family closer to each other and to God.

- Answers to problems come easily if they are other people's problems.

- Some problems can be attacked; others must be endured. All problems should be given to God.

- The best way to reduce the size of your troubles is to compare them to the size of your blessings.

Divorce is an easy escape, many think. But in counseling many divorcées, the guilt and loneliness they experience can be even more tragic than living with their problem.

= 62 =

DIVORCE

We are living in an age of disposability. Everything from diapers to cameras to contact lenses can be used and then discarded. After we use them once—or when we are tired of them—we toss them. With this type of mentality, we don't often place sentimental (or even practical) significance on many of the things in our lives. Sadly, this perspective has invaded our society's view of marriage, with the predictable result of divorce.

God intends marriage to be permanent. Jesus Himself said that since a husband and wife "are no longer two but one, let no one separate them, for God has joined them together" (Matthew 19:6 NLT). This means that young couples might have to change their perspective about marriage before they enter it. They should not view marriage as a hobby that can be tried and abandoned when their interest in it (or in each other) wanes.

And for those already in marriage, they need to work as hard at keeping the marriage together as they worked to get married in the first place. For them divorce should not even be an option, and they need to sense God's desire that they make every effort toward continual and mutual forgiveness and restoration.

But for many people, divorce has already occurred in their lives. Are they doomed to experience less than a good life because of their failed marriage? Just because they have chosen (or had forced upon them) a circumstance that is not God's preference, they are not stuck living in an inferior "Plan B" world. God does not reserve His love only for those who follow His intended "Plan A." And aren't we glad of that, because every one of us has stepped outside of Plan A. We may not all have been divorced, but we have all disappointed and failed God. And while God hates divorce, He also hates our lying, and our pride, and any disrespect or unkindness we show to our spouse even if we remain married.

We have a God who is in the business of restoring relationships. The most *important* relationship is ours with Him. While we can reject Him quickly and frequently, He is always ready to forgive and receive us back into fellowship with Him. He never abandons us. He never quits on us. He never gives up on us.

God's unconditional love is the model He wants us to

use for marriage. So, in our age of disposability, let's not look at marriages as something that can be discarded or recycled.

...In the Small Stuff

- Keep looking for ways to restore your marriage instead of looking for reasons to leave it.
- If a marriage was founded only on love at first sight, it is likely to end by divorce at first thought.
- Some people give more thought to choosing a divorce attorney than to restoring their marriage.

Shew me thy ways, O LORD;
teach me thy paths.
PSALM 25:4 KJV

= 63 =

EDUCATION

The importance of education cannot be overemphasized. But people often confuse schooling with education. There are some similarities, but there are some significant differences.

Schooling usually ends after twelve to sixteen years. You start at kindergarten and you stop when you get your diploma. But an education should be a continual, lifelong process. You begin learning as a child, and hopefully the process doesn't ever stop. If you have an attitude of learning throughout your life, then you stay inquisitive. Boredom won't be a worry for you if you are always looking to acquire knowledge about new subjects.

Schooling usually has a set of curricula; there are established subjects and majors. You may have some electives, but your choices are limited to what is offered by the school. Your education, however, has no such limitations. Your education is limited only by your own curiosity.

Schooling happens in the classroom, but your education is not limited to what you learn within the four walls of an educational institution.

Schooling often focuses on learning from textbooks, but an education can be gained from life itself. In the classroom, you might learn historical facts or mathematical formulas. Your education includes what you can learn from people, places, and circumstances.

Schooling is not a family activity, but education can be. Many lessons about life can be learned during family activities. In this context, opportunities will arise to learn (and teach) lessons about relationships, attitudes, and perspectives.

When you consider that God has the events in your life under His watchful eye, you realize that He can bring into your life the things that you need to learn. Of course, you need to be living life with the expectation of learning from it. Look at life as an opportunity to obtain the education that God has in store for you. After all, what you learn in life is tuition-free.

. . .In the Small Stuff

- Be a student of life.
- In every new and difficult situation, ask yourself: "What can I learn from this?"
- The more you learn about God, the more you will learn about yourself.

*"Wherever your treasure is, there your heart
and thought will also be."*
MATTHEW 6:21 NLT

= 64 =

MONEY MANAGEMENT

You can talk about what is important to you, but your true priorities will be revealed by how you handle your finances. And those around you may not pay attention to what you are saying, but they will certainly notice how you spend your money. This can be a real case of cash receipts talking louder than words.

Your personal finances are, in fact, a convenient way to judge the kind of person you are. A brief examination of your spending habits may disclose more about you than you wish to know:

- You might consider yourself to be generous, but that is not really the case if you can walk by the Salvation Army Christmas donation bucket without flinching.

- Maybe you think that you are free from material-ism, but that probably isn't the case if you have the Home Shopping Channel toll-free number on your phone's speed dial.
- And you aren't very charitable if you turn off the lights in the house and don't answer the doorbell when the Girl Scouts come to sell cookies.

Not only do your finances provide you with a mirror to your heart, they also provide you with an excellent teaching tool. As with many aspects of life, your conduct can be a good example or a poor one. Fortunately, we can choose what kind of example we wish to be. So, for example, if we want to reflect that God has priority in our life, then we will want to acknowledge that priority by returning some of our wealth to Him. Now, He doesn't need it, and we can't make a check directly payable to "God" (or if we do, we aren't really sincere because we know it won't get cashed), but there are ministries that can use our money to help the poor.

Self-reflection and self-examination from time to time are good things. But don't just contemplate yourself in your mind. Actually pull out that checkbook and see where you have been spending your money. It will be time well spent to determine if your money was well spent.

- True charity doesn't care if it is tax-deductible.

- Don't give to God because He needs it. Give to God because He deserves it.

- Whether you have a lot or a little, the quality of your life is not determined by the quantity in your life.

Few things help an individual more than to
place responsibility upon him,
and to let him know that you trust him.
BOOKER T. WASHINGTON

= 65 =

RESPONSIBILITIES

Living in a family brings responsibilities to everyone. Many families only think of the parents as having responsibilities, but that is a huge mistake. If children don't learn to accept and assume responsibility at a young age, they will be more apt to avoid it when they are older.

Why are parents often remiss when it comes to teaching responsibility to their children? We can think of two possible reasons:

- Some parents think that the imposition of responsibilities will alienate their children. Parents are concerned about protecting their children from negative influences. They worry about what their children are doing, and whom they are doing it with. These parents recognize that their children often come close to crossing the line of acceptable behavior and friends. Out of fear that their children might rebel against assigned chores and duties, these parents abstain from assigning responsibilities to their children. What a tragedy, and what a contradiction! In an attempt to protect their children, these parents are not preparing their children for the future. These children are left vulnerable and ill-prepared to accept and shoulder the responsibilities they will find in their future jobs and families.

• Some parents may be too busy to impose responsibilities upon their children. Time is required to give your children chores and assignments: adequate explanation and instruction takes time; monitoring their performance takes time; evaluating the quality of their work takes time; and time is required for rewards (or discipline) as appropriate. But in many families, parental time is in short supply. It may be easier, and certainly quicker, to "do it yourself" or "not do it at all" than to assign it to the children. But this attitude places a higher value on the parent's time than on the child's character. Time will always be limited, but the opportunity for building the character of your child is fleeting.

Responsibility is a character trait that will produce strong families (and a strong society). But responsibility doesn't happen by accident. It isn't acquired from a parent's wishful thinking or good intentions. Responsibility comes as the result of years of character training. It is developed gradually. If it is not nurtured in your home, you will be stunting your child's growth.

. . .IN THE SMALL STUFF

- Only a few people take responsibility; the rest of them just want to take the credit.
- Accountability to God produces responsibility in life.
- Your children's success or failure in life will be determined in large part by how they handle their responsibilities.

Be strong and of a good courage.
DEUTERONOMY 31:23 KJV

= 66 =

ENCOURAGEMENT

Most people think that encouragement is nothing more than positive words spoken to uplift, comfort, and inspire. Well, that's partly correct. But sincere and effective encouragement must be more than a vocabulary list of motivational terminology gleaned from one of those infomercial salesmen with an overactive thyroid gland.

If you want your encouragement to be effective, it must be honest. Don't try to motivate your child with false praise about being the best player on the team if there is a permanent indentation on the bench where your child sat all season long. Your children will not be encouraged by comments they know are dishonest. In fact, it will make them feel even worse. They will assume they are so worthless that you are forced to lie to think of something good to say about them.

You should always be ready with a word of encouragement

when it is needed, but you shouldn't be cavalier about it. Effective encouragement might require quite a bit of creativity on your part. You have to know exactly what to say. . .and how to say it. . .and when to say it. In times of discouragement, your family members may be particularly sensitive and defensive. Timing and phrasing are important. An encouraging word, spoken at the wrong time or with the wrong inflection, might be misinterpreted as sarcasm or criticism.

Effective encouragement also requires a proper environment. Encouragement doesn't come naturally in homes where there is hostility and cynicism. In an antagonistic environment, people are too wrapped up in tearing each other down to bother with building each other up. In contrast, a loving home *fosters* encouragement. In that type of environment, your family will feel secure and appreciated. When a loving attitude pervades the home, each family member is encouraged without words even being spoken because they have a sense of self-worth. . .they know they are loved by their family and by God because of *who* they are and not because of *what* they have accomplished. They are free to tackle new challenges, and free to fail in the attempt, because they are fully confident that they will have the support of their family.

As you think about encouraging your family, don't rely just on words. Look for other ways to communicate what you want to say. Remember, sometimes your heart needs to speak louder than your mouth.

- Encouragement is anatomical: a pat on the back and a kick in the rear to lift the chin and straighten the shoulders.

- Correction is instructional; encouragement is motivational.

- Encouragement costs nothing, and yet it pays tremendous dividends.

If you refuse to discipline your children,
it proves you don't love them;
if you love your children,
you will be prompt to discipline them.
PROVERBS 13:24 NLT

DISCIPLINE

Many families are so contemporary that they no longer practice what has become the lost art of our ancestors. No, we aren't talking about quilting. Somewhere in
the past few decades we have lost the art of child discipline.
Oh, it's not that we have abandoned the concept of discipline altogether. But we apply it selectively. We love discipline as a "positive mental attitude" (such as "I won't tell
my son he can't use my cell phone as a toy because I don't
want to squelch his curiosity."). But we have pretty much
abandoned any politically incorrect concept of correcting a
child's misbehavior with discipline (such as "I won't tell my
son he can't dismantle the television set because I wouldn't

want to squelch his innate curiosity").

Although the concept may seem old-fashioned, the Bible says that parents who love their children will discipline them. It is a vital part of parental responsibility. Without correction, children will grow up with no clear understanding of behavioral boundaries. A lack of discipline suggests that the parents have little regard for the child's character development.

Many parents are reluctant to discipline because they don't want to stifle their child's creativity. This philosophy, however, shows a misunderstanding of behavior and discipline. Discipline is for the purpose of developing the child's sense of good and evil, right and wrong. Some behavior, although creative, is just plain wrong and needs to be stifled. But discipline does not require inactivity. In fact, discipline should not convey that "good" means immobility and "evil" means activity. It is not the goal of discipline to produce sedate and passive children. Discipline should channel creativity and enthusiasm into productive and beneficial activities.

No one ever said that child discipline was easy (and now, it is not even socially acceptable). It takes time and patience to design a plan of discipline that will teach and correct your children without exasperating them or causing them to be angry or discouraged. And just when you find a technique that works, they outgrow it, and you have to go back to the discipline drawing board.

Take heart! Your consistent, loving discipline will ultimately teach your children to discipline themselves. Then your job will be easier.

- Early discipline averts future disaster.

- It is better for a parent to impose limits when children are young than for a judge to impose a sentence when they are older.

- Sometimes "learning at your mother's knee" requires being bent over it.

They were amazed at his teaching, for [Jesus]
taught as one who had real authority.
MARK 1:22 NLT

= 68 =

AUTHORITY

Your household can't run efficiently without someone in charge. There needs to be a chain of command. Someone has got to be in charge. However, the question of "Who's the Boss?" can be a point of contention that disrupts the harmony in your home.

Our humble suggestion is that you let God be the authority in your home. We know that sounds trite and is easy to say, but it is exactly the arrangement God designed. Notice the ramifications of this approach.

On issues of disagreement between a husband and wife, neither one gets to have it "his way" or "her way." There won't be the drawing of battle lines. There won't be one winner and one loser. Instead, both the husband and wife can agree to see what God has to say about the issue.

Of course, God won't always speak specifically to each issue. (For instance, He probably won't tell you whether you should buy a Toyota instead of a Honda.) But the Bible has clear guidelines in many practical areas, such as money management. And even if the answer to a specific question can't be found in the Bible, God can work in the hearts and minds of the husband and wife as they pray and read the Bible together. They submit to the authority of God in their family when they are willing to accept His decision (instead of their own) on the issue.

Placing God as the authority in the home has an advantage for parents. The parents don't have to become the final arbiters on many issues. Instead, the family can agree that they will look to God (through the Bible) to decide contested issues. The Bible speaks clearly on issues such as behavior, attitude, and influences. Parents and children often have a difference of opinion on these issues, and either one could be taking an extreme position. Instead of arguing, they should agree to see if God has anything to say on the issue and, if so, to let that be the final decision. In addition to finding the answer, both the parent and child will spiritually benefit from the practice of submitting to God's authority.

When God is the authority in the home, your family can be a partnership of equals. Oh sure, the husband, wife, and children will have different roles, but they can trust each other, knowing that each person functions in the family under God's leadership and authority.

- Some people handle authority well and grow in the process; others misuse authority and just overinflate.

- It is better to learn submission to authority in the backyard than the prison yard.

- Authority in the home is like a bottle of fine wine. It increases in value if you don't have to use it.

Trust in the LORD with all your heart;
do not depend on your own understanding.
Seek his will in all you do,
and he will direct your paths.
PROVERBS 3:5–6 NLT

= 69 =

DECISION MAKING

You should protect your children from many things, but don't protect them so much that they miss the opportunity to make decisions. Decision making is a skill that must be developed. And part of the learning process includes making a few wrong decisions. Isn't it better to allow your children to make a few "wrong decisions" when the consequences are relatively minor and you are around to assist in the learning process? Don't let your children's first confrontation and struggle with major decisions come after they have left home.

The best way to teach your children about decision making is to model it for them. Let them watch you go through the process. Of course, this means you have to let them know a little bit about what's going on in the family (and that might not be too bad either). The decision might be as momentous as whether you should change careers, or it could be as mundane as whether to buy a new car. (Of course, you can have a little fun with this. Tell your teenagers you're thinking about buying a car, and they'll get all excited. Then tell them the car is a 1986 Chrysler LeBaron, and watch their faces go pale.) The important point is to let them see how you approach the decision…whether you make a list of the "pros" and "cons," or whether you research information, or whether you ask the advice of others. (Of course, this presupposes that you actually have a process for making decisions. If you don't, then that's your mistake, and your children can learn the consequences of random selection.)

Including your child in the process is the best *method* to teach them decision making, but the most important *principle* to teach them about decision making is to include God in the process. Don't let them think that God is only interested in the major decisions of life. ("What job should I take?" "Whom should I marry?") Show them that God is interested in the smallest details of their lives. Just as you care *where* they go, *who* they're with, and *what* they're doing, so does God. And He is available to guide them in each of those daily decisions that they will be making.

At some point, your children will be on their own facing significant decisions. You probably won't be available (or asked) to give your opinion. But you can do something *now* that will help your children *then*. Let them make some of their own decisions now, so they can learn that God needs to be part of the process.

- Freedom is the ability to make decisions. Wisdom is the ability to make the right decisions.

- Your children won't learn how to make the right decisions unless you give them enough freedom to make the wrong ones.

- Decisions made too quickly can leave you stuck with consequences that last a lifetime.

*"You promised me, Lord, that if I followed
You, You would walk with me always. But
I have noticed that during the most trying
periods of my life there has only been one set
of footprints in the sand. Why, when I needed
You most, have You not been there for me?"
The Lord replied, "The years when you have
seen only one set of footprints, My child,
is when I carried you."*

FROM "FOOTPRINTS IN THE SAND," AUTHOR UNKNOWN

"WHY, GOD, WHY?"

When things are going well in your life, everything seems
good with the world:

- The sun shines brighter.

- The flowers are more fragrant.

- People smile as they pass by you.

- There is a vacant parking spot for you directly in
  front of Starbucks.

Of course, things aren't really that way, but that's how they seem to you because you're feeling good about your situation.

When your circumstances turn south, though, there seems to be an odd confluence with the rest of the cosmos. Everything seems to sour simultaneously:

- You get soaking wet after being caught in a freak rain storm.

- You get a flat tire and don't have a jack in the trunk.

- Everyone who crosses your path is in a foul mood.

- After waiting fifteen minutes in the drive-thru at Starbucks, you are informed that they are out of coffee.

It's bad enough that [insert your tragedy here] happened to you—but to make things worse, it became a triggering mechanism for further misfortune.

These are trivial illustrations of how your perspective is corrupted when you are forced to endure a tragic circumstance or a particularly hard situation. But more than your attitude is affected by adversity. Your spiritual equilibrium can also be thrown off kilter. Often, the frustration that accompanies your hardship leads to a spiritual misconception: *God has abandoned you.* While this isn't true, it is easy to see how you can reach this flawed conclusion. First, you start with sound premises, such as:

- God is the almighty Creator and Ruler of the universe.
- All things are under His sovereign control.
- Nothing happens in the world without His knowledge or permission.
- God loves you and wants only what is best for you.

So far, your theology is on track. But here is the point where your logic slips a cog. You mistakenly conclude:

- Since tragedy has entered your life, God must have turned His back on you.
- If He really loved you, He wouldn't let this happen to you.

This line of thinking is flawed. First, God never promises anyone a life free from pain. So don't make the mistake of thinking that God has abandoned you when hardship enters your life. Secondly, the *presence of hardship* in your life does not imply the *absence of God* in your life. To the contrary, you can be sure that God is there and wants to reveal Himself to you when you are experiencing difficulties.

Rather than approaching your tough times with the attitude that God has vanished, use these circumstances to find God. He is there. And He isn't hiding. He wants you to feel His presence. He wants you to sense His love for you. He desires for you to understand His purposes for allowing these difficulties in your life.

God is with you. Yes, He is all-powerful and capable of changing the hard circumstances of your life. But because He loves you and wants what is best for you, He will not eliminate those problems if He knows they serve a beneficial purpose in your life. He never promised to protect you from all hurt, but He has promised to be by your side during every bit of it.

If you mistakenly assume that God is not present, you'll be spiritually blind to His presence. But if you take God at His word and expect to find Him in the darkest hours, you'll be surprised that you see Him all around you. Suddenly, the severity of your problems will shrink in comparison to the magnitude of God's presence in your life.

. . .In the Small Stuff

- God doesn't remove the difficulty and pain. But He will be there with you through it all.

- God's continual presence with you is one of His presents to you.

- How do you expect to recognize God during times of crisis if you haven't been taking notice of Him when things are going well?

Complete success alienates a man from his
fellows, but suffering makes kinsmen of us all.
ELBERT HUBBARD

= 71 =

INNOCENT SUFFERING

Of all the types of suffering we see in the world, the most difficult to understand often is the suffering that happens when natural disasters occur. After a while, all the tragedies seem to run together—the hurricane in New Orleans, the tsunami in Asia, the earthquakes in Japan and Haiti—leaving many of us numb to the misery they create.

You can't help but feel a sense of helplessness when such disasters occur. Because they originate with this planet we call home, we all feel the sting when the earth convulses. And we wonder: can we trust this life-giving sphere that is usually so good to us? It all seems rather capricious, especially when those who are least able to handle the terrestrial blast of earthquakes, typhoons, and floods are often hit the hardest.

How do we deal with this kind of suffering? What are

our options? We can believe that nature has run amok and out of God's control. Or we can believe that nature is all there is, with no God to care or wield any authoritative restraint. Those are the options of people who have given up on God. They aren't very comforting, are they? If nature is the beginning and the end of all things, and if we are merely pawns in a mindless game of chance and natural selection (it's survival of the fittest, you know), there is no need to wonder why we suffer—because there is no explanation.

People who still hold to a belief in some kind of God—and most of the world operates this way—look beyond nature for answers. Even in this realm of belief, there are multiple views. One is that God is using nature to inflict punishment on His wayward created beings. He did it once—remember the Great Flood?—and He can do it again. Ah, but there's the rainbow, God's promise to humankind that He will never inflict such worldwide harm again:

> *"I will never again curse the earth, destroying all living things, even though people's thoughts and actions are bent toward evil from childhood. As long as the earth remains, there will be springtime and harvest, cold and heat, winter and summer, day and night."*
>
> GENESIS 8:21–22 NLT

We must look elsewhere for some kind of explanation, though none can be found to satisfy everyone. Perhaps a partial answer is found in the New Testament. In his letter to the first-century Roman church, the apostle Paul wrote:

All creation anticipates the day when it will join God's children in glorious freedom from death and decay. For we know that all creation has been groaning as in the pains of childbirth right up to the present time.

ROMANS 8:21–22 NLT

Even creation is under the weight of sin and suffering, brought into this world by rebellious acts of the people God made. It isn't that God has lost control; He is merely allowing His creation to operate in the physical world He made for us, functioning superbly and incredibly 99.9 percent of the time. Occasionally, though, it groans from the contractions that will someday result in a new heaven and a new earth.

Meanwhile, we must also groan—with compassion—for those affected by Earth's sometimes unexplainable behavior. If we are to find meaning in any of this, we should find it in the help we can give to those who suffer.

. . . IN THE SMALL STUFF

- God has taken extraordinary measures to provide a comfortable and beneficial place for us to live.

- God does not cause suffering, but He allows it to happen for reasons we don't always understand.

- Never allow your own comfort to keep you from giving comfort to others.

It is easier to bear some abuse if I reflect,
"I do not deserve this reproach but I do
deserve others that have not been made."
Francois Mauriac

= 72 =

WHEN LIFE DOESN'T SEEM FAIR

No one likes tough times, but difficulties are even tougher to take if their imposition seems unfair. There appear to be three levels for determining whether hardship is deserved or undeserved:

- Level 1—I deserve it. Much of the time, we can't blame the devil—or God—for the problems that enter our lives. Often those difficult circumstances are just the natural and inevitable result of our poor choices or foolish behavior.

- Level 2—I don't deserve it, but it's a part of life. We live in a broken world, with rampant evil, illness, and natural disasters. No one is immune from misfortune. If you are hoping to avoid trouble, the odds are against you. As a resident of Planet Earth, sooner or later it is going to get you.

- Level 3—I was doing something good, and this is the thanks I get? Sometimes trouble comes your way when you're being nice to someone else or engaged in a good cause.

At Level 1, bad things happen to bad people; your struggles are compensatory—you brought them on yourself. At Level 2, bad things happen to good people; your strife is undeserved, but at least it is understandable, so you endure it. But Level 3 is the hardest to rationalize; this is when bad things happen to good people when they are doing good things.

It doesn't seem right that undeserved grief should be heaped upon you when you are engaged in a noble effort. But it happens:

- You stand up for a coworker who is unjustly criticized, and you lose your job for insubordination.

- You have been caring for an infirm parent for many years. It has been a thankless and exhausting job. To protect your own sanity and provide better care at a critical stage, you make the difficult decision to opt for a nursing home. Your adult siblings, all of whom live out-of-state and have never offered any assistance, accuse you of being selfish and heartless.

- You take the right stand on a black and white moral issue, but the offending party manipulates the situation and you become the bad guy.

Here is the irony of it all. You got involved only because you are a good person. Anyone with less character would have remained on the sidelines; the spineless ones are safe and unscathed. But because of your integrity, you were compelled to enter the fray. You were willing to sacrifice time and energy and emotion. In light of what you were willing to give—which others were not—you should have gotten a reward. Instead, you gained nothing but undeserved grief.

But you didn't engage in your noble act for the sake of a reward. You did it because it was the right thing to do. And that's the perspective you need to maintain when you suffer for doing good. God honors those who do what is right. He has mercy on those who are defenseless. You can thank God that He has wired you in such a way that you cannot stand idly by in the face of injustice or wrongdoing. If God created you to take a stand for the cause of right, you can be assured that He will rescue you from the accompanying fallout.

. . .IN THE SMALL STUFF

- Sometimes the criticism of others affirms the propriety of your action.

- Those who don't have the courage to respond often have the nerve to complain.

- Integrity means doing what is right, even when it isn't popular. Popularity allows you to live with others, but integrity lets you live with yourself.

There's something about resurrections
that requires crosses.
ROBERT SLOAN

= 73 =

WHERE IS GOD WHEN WE SUFFER?

It's so easy to shake our fists at God when something extraordinarily painful happens to us. The most natural question to ask is, "Where is God in all of this?" Maybe you have asked, *Where is God in my cancer? Where is God in my father's stroke? Where is God in my baby's birth defect?*

Maybe you've asked the question in less physical situations that are no less painful. You could be going through a nasty divorce. One of your children could be disrupting your entire household through his or her poor choices. Or you could be the victim of corporate downsizing, creating an unbearable financial strain. Where is God in all of this? Hasn't He promised an abundant life to His children? Doesn't He care when we hurt?

Yes, God does care. He cares so much that it cost Him

the life of His only Son. You see, when we think that God neither cares about us nor identifies with our suffering and hurts, we forget that the Son of God suffered beyond what any of us can even imagine. From the beginning of His ministry on earth, Jesus knew what He had to do: bear the cumulative sin and sickness and evil and disease and pain of the entire human race. This was the incredible burden Jesus carried. It was His mission, and He knew it (Matthew 16:21).

No wonder, then, that when Jesus was praying in the Garden of Gethsemane He asked the Father to release Him from the terrible task at hand. "Yet I want your will, not mine," He said (Matthew 26:39 NLT). We know that God's will was for Jesus to suffer and die so that we would have the opportunity to live. We may not understand it, but suffering—most significantly the suffering of Christ— is God's way of fixing what went wrong when sin entered and nearly destroyed the world.

When we ask, "Where is God when we suffer?" we need only look to Christ, who suffered for us so that ultimately, in the life that follows this temporal existence, we won't have to suffer. Meanwhile, we live imperfectly in an imperfect world. We see through a glass darkly, knowing that someday our tears and pain will be removed. . .for good. When we do suffer—as long as we aren't suffering for something that comes from our own poor choices—we can take comfort in knowing that we are "partners with Christ" in His suffering (1 Peter 4:13 NLT).

As people who walk this earth with a heavenly perspective,

suffering is both our curse and our calling. We may not like it or understand why, but we know there is Someone who has gone before us and promises never to leave us.

. . .IN THE SMALL STUFF

- Never forget that God knows firsthand what it's like to suffer.

- God's will is not always the easiest, but it is always the best.

- Sometimes God chooses the most unlikely methods to accomplish His purposes.

Lord, on You I call for help against my blind
and senseless torment, since You alone can
renew inwardly and outwardly my mind,
my will, and my strength, which are weak.
MICHELANGELO

= 74 =

YOU'RE NOT EXEMPT

There are certain privileges that accompany association:

- If you are a member of AAA, you get hotel discounts.

- If you are affiliated with an airline's frequent flyer club, you accumulate bonus miles for free travel.

- If you work at McDonald's, you might get to eat the french fries left over at closing time.

- If you are a sales clerk at JCPenney, you get an employee discount on clothing.

- If your spouse is in law enforcement, the highway patrol officer might let you off with a warning when you've been doing eighty mph in a seventy zone.

Many people think there are comparable "exclusive membership benefits" if they associate with God. They think there is some providential protection that surrounds everyone who believes in Him. They believe a guardian angel guarantee will protect them from trouble, tragedy, and turmoil. Too bad for them—they must not have read the fine print in their celestial contract.

The fact that God does not insulate those He loves from pain and suffering should be evident. For example, consider Jesus—who had a *very* close association with God. God allowed Jesus to suffer. And if you are unclear about that, just watch *The Passion of the Christ* movie. (The word *passion* used in this context refers to suffering.) But Jesus wasn't alone in His suffering. According to ancient tradition, most of His close followers endured torture and/or a painful death:

- Stephen and Matthew were martyred.
- Luke and Philip were both hanged.
- Peter and Simeon were crucified.
- Mark was dragged to his death in the streets of Alexandria.
- John was dunked into a pot of boiling water.
- Bartholomew was killed by having his skin ripped off while he was still alive.

All of these men loved God. But if you were God's P.R. agent, these are not the stories you would put in a recruiting brochure. Their treatment runs contrary to our notion that

God shelters those He loves from harm. Well, that notion is flat-out wrong. Our tendency is to decorate our concepts of God with thoughts of love and peace and "blessings." It's true that God is about all those things. But that is a limited and one-dimensional understanding of His nature. We must expand our understanding of God—including a realization that He considers troubles to be a blessing. That's why the Bible says we are to rejoice when hardships come our way:

> *Dear brothers and sisters, whenever trouble comes your way, let it be an opportunity for joy. For when your faith is tested, your endurance has a chance to grow. So let it grow, for when your endurance is fully developed, you will be strong in character and ready for anything.*
>
> JAMES 1:2–4 NLT

God doesn't want us to rejoice in suffering simply because He has a perverse sense of humor. He wants us to realize that our struggles drive us closer to Him. Difficulties are a necessary component for building the foundation of our faith. They cause us to seek God, because we might otherwise tend to ignore Him in tranquil circumstances. They impress upon us our need for God. They expose our lack of self-sufficiency, and we become convinced of our dependency on Him.

The next time difficulties come your way, don't say, "I love God. . .this shouldn't be happening to me." Instead, realize that those circumstances haven't escaped God's notice. He loves you and can use such situations for your good.

- Easy times may make you spiritually indifferent, but hard times make you spiritually dependent. And that is exactly how God wants you.

- Loving God doesn't exempt you from troubles, but it does ensure that you won't go through them alone.

- The Bible says to rejoice in your troubles. That means that when life gets bad, you've still got something good going on.

*Yet what we suffer now is nothing compared
to the glory he will give us later.*
ROMANS 8:18 NLT

= 75 =

THANKING GOD

Is it possible to thank God when we hurt? Is it possible to thank God when we observe the suffering of others? Not only is it possible, it's advisable. When we fail to acknowledge God in our suffering, we fail to understand why we are able to get through it.

You may not feel like thanking God in the midst of your suffering, and certainly you don't want to thank God when a disaster strikes someone else but misses you. That's not what we're talking about. Thanking God when we hurt goes much deeper.

Thanking God in our suffering means that we can thank Him for getting us *through* our suffering. Have you ever been surprised by how much pain you can endure? When you were very young, it didn't take much to make you cry. A pinched finger or an unkind word was usually enough to get the tears flowing. But through the years you have toughened up. You can handle more pain, especially if it means helping to ease the pain of someone else.

The apostle Paul experienced more than his share of pain and suffering. He was beaten on many occasions, shipwrecked, and thrown in prison several times. Once Paul was bitten by a poisonous snake! He didn't ignore or try to minimize his problems; Paul was very aware of the trials he had endured. Even more, he was aware of his resilience in the face of overwhelming odds. In his letter to the Corinthian church, he wrote:

> *We are pressed on every side by troubles, but we are not crushed and broken. We are perplexed, but we don't give up and quit. We are hunted down, but God never abandons us. We get knocked down, but we get up again and keep going.*
>
> 2 Corinthians 4:8–9 nlt

Paul's determination reminds us of Winston Churchill, whose most famous speech was also his shortest and most powerful. As Adolf Hitler was threatening to overrun England and Western Europe, Churchill said to a group of students:

> *Never give in—never, never, never, never, in nothing great or small, large or petty, never give in except to convictions of honour and good sense. Never yield to force; never yield to the apparently overwhelming might of the enemy.*

No doubt there have been times when you gritted your teeth and snarled in the face of adversity. Where does this determination come from? It can come from only one source—our Creator, who built into every person the strength to overcome adversity.

Like Paul, we may feel crushed and broken—but we aren't! We may not know why certain things are happening to us, but we don't give up. We can thank God for what many have called the indomitable human spirit. And we can thank God for never, ever abandoning us.

There's another sense in which we can thank God in our suffering. When things get so bad that we don't think we can bear it any longer, there is someone we can count on to help ease our burden. His name is Jesus, the One who suffered for us more than we will ever know. He is the One who makes our life possible.

Jesus once spoke to a group of people, many of whom were just like us—burdened and hurting. He offered words of comfort that are just as real now as they were two thousand years ago:

> *"Come to me, all of you who are weary and carry heavy burdens, and I will give you rest. Take my yoke upon you. Let me teach you, because I am humble and gentle, and you will find rest for your souls. For my yoke fits perfectly, and the burden I give you is light."*
>
> MATTHEW 11:28–30 NLT

God has made you to endure and overcome suffering, and Jesus promises to help carry your heavy load. That's why we can be thankful in our suffering.

. . .IN THE SMALL STUFF

- Thanking God in everything will help you get through anything.
- Your ability to handle adversity comes from the God who has overcome adversity.
- God will never, never, never, never abandon you.

Job stood up and tore his robe in grief. Then he shaved his head and fell to the ground before God. He said, "I came naked from my mother's womb, and I will be stripped of everything when I die. The LORD gave me everything I had, and the LORD has taken it away. Praise the name of the LORD!" In all of this, Job did not sin by blaming God.

JOB 1:20–22 NLT

= 76 =

THE STORY OF JOB

It was a cosmic challenge that occurred approximately four thousand years ago. Satan alleged that Job was a faithful follower of God only because God had blessed Job with great prosperity. God knew better, but He allowed Satan to "test" Job by intervening in the circumstances of Job's life and decimating his idyllic situation. Unbeknownst to him, Job was about to endure a real-life riches-to-rags drama. Literally within moments, Job received news that:

- a band of desert marauders had stolen his oxen and donkeys and killed his farmhands;
- all of his sheep and shepherds were killed in a freak fire storm;
- raiders had stolen his camels and murdered his servants; and
- a fierce windstorm caused the collapse of a house that killed all of his sons and daughters.

To add further distress in Job's time of grief, Satan struck him with festering boils from his head to his feet. But in all of this tragedy, Job did not blame God.

Job's wife found him sitting in a pile of rubble and ashes, scraping his sores with a piece of broken pottery. While theologians through the ages have criticized her for a lack of faith in God's sovereignty, she seemed to respond with natural, human emotions when she yelled at Job, saying, "Are you still maintaining an allegiance to God? Get over it. Just curse God and die!" (see Job 2:9).

At this point in the story we learn a valuable lesson from Job. He disclosed to his wife a perspective on life— the perspective of how he could worship God in the midst of adversity with the same intensity and reverence that he had during times of prosperity:

> *"Should we accept only good things from the hand of God and never anything bad?"*
>
> JOB 2:10 NLT

This question is simply profound, and profoundly simple: It is easy to trust God with the oversight of our lives when we are enjoying the ride. But shouldn't we also trust Him when the going gets hard? Even when it gets *very hard*? After all, doesn't God know what we need in our lives to achieve His purposes? Why do we suppose that He should be restricted to using only pleasant circumstances?

Like Job's wife, we often make the mistake of constructing a paradigm that assumes God can work in our lives only through prosperity. Job saw through that faulty logic. If we anticipate (and desire) that God is accomplishing His will in our lives, then we must factor into our life's equation the *ways* in which God works. Those ways are many and varied. He works through His Word, the Bible. He works through other people. And He can work through any succession of enjoyable circumstances, from the mundane to the miraculous: a salary increase, moving into a new home, a reconciled relationship, the birth of a baby, or the recovery from a significant health problem.

But God's way may also include a succession of unpleasant events, even catastrophes: the loss of a job, the foreclosure on your home, a breakup of a valued relationship, the birth of a deformed child, or the diagnosis of a fatal disease.

Like Job, we need to come into a deeper understanding of how God works. When we appreciate that God uses the tough times in our lives, it will make those circumstances easier to endure. But that isn't the entire benefit of Job's perspective. There is the added bonus that we will begin to see God at work in those difficult situations. All of a sudden, life's challenges aren't simply something to be endured. We can begin to see them as tools God is using to shape our lives for the better—and we can see God as the Master Craftsman skillfully using those tools to shape us according to His design. That's why after Job had endured more suffering than most of us could ever conceive, he was able to say to God:

> *"I had heard about you before, but now I have seen you with my own eyes."*
>
> JOB 42:5 NLT

. . .IN THE SMALL STUFF

- Try to see God in the tough times with the same clarity that you see Him in the fun times.
- You can curse God and die, or you can find a reason for living in what He brings your way.
- Don't let the secret of Job's life go undiscovered in your life.

Prayer is not conquering God's reluctance,
but taking hold of God's willingness.
PHILLIPS BROOKS

= 77 =

WHEN PRAYER DOESN'T SEEM TO WORK

Satan often plays an insidious trick on people of faith. During times of difficulty in their lives, he gets them to wonder whether their prayers to God have any effect. Consider how this ploy can escalate your feelings of discouragement and despair:

- You are already dealing with challenging struggles in your life. You come to the point where you are at the end of your resources. God is your only help.

- If heaven-sent relief doesn't come immediately, you begin to wonder whether your prayers are hitting the ceiling and stopping there. Even if they blast through the insulation in the attic and reach God, is He paying attention to them?

- If God is the only answer to your problem, and if He isn't being attentive to your situation, then it seems to you that you are doomed.

- So, in addition to the misery you are enduring, you now become spiritually despondent. With a fatalistic attitude, you simply give up. At precisely the time you should be praying the most, you stop all conversations with God because prayer seems to be an exercise in futility.

In circumstances such as this, the fault is not God's. The ineffectiveness of our prayers is often the fault of our own misunderstanding of the nature of God. To state it more succinctly: with bad theology, we pray in vain.

The essence of effective prayer is determined by our concept of whom we are praying to. If we are praying to an all-knowing, all-loving, and all-powerful God, then His response will make sense. But if we are praying to a puny God, then it is no wonder that His replies seem useless to us.

When our prayer life falters, a false impression of God is frequently the culprit. We are not fully convinced of

- *His love.* Does God really care about me? Am I important to Him? There are so many people who are better than I am, so why would God love me?

- *His power.* Is God able to solve the problems I'm experiencing? Is He capable of intervening in all of the complicated, interconnected circumstances of my life to fully rectify the difficulties? My situation requires more than a quick fix; is God really up to the task?

- *His wisdom.* Does God know what is best for me? I'm in the middle of it, and I'm not even sure of the solution. Can I trust God's judgment? What if His opinion of what is best doesn't match with mine?

If you could be objective—looking at these issues without the pressure of present adversity in your life—you would know the answers to these questions. But, understandably, current misfortune has knocked your theology off track. So let's put the misconceptions to rest: the Bible says that God's love, power, and wisdom are infinite; they are perfect, and they are all focused on you. But if you doubt any of them, your prayers are hindered—not because God is rendered ineffective, but because you are not adequately prepared to accept His response.

Disappointment in prayer is usually caused by our failure to believe that He loves us, that He is fully capable of handling the circumstances of our lives, or that He knows what is best for us.

If your prayers have seemed ineffective, don't give up on prayer—and don't give up on God. Realize that you hold the top position on His "to do" list. Know that He is able to do exceedingly more than you can imagine. And finally, trust Him; acknowledge that His wisdom is greater than yours. His resolution of the situation may be different than what you expect—in timing and results—but it will be better than what you have in mind.

What are you waiting for? Give prayer another chance. But this time, properly consider the One to whom you are praying.

- If your prayers aren't working, make sure you are praying to the God who is all-loving, all-powerful, and all-knowing.

- Don't expect God to answer your prayers if you don't really believe He can do anything about them.

- There is a time and place for prayer: anytime and anyplace.

In His will is our peace.
DANTE ALIGHIERI

= 78 =

HOW TO KNOW GOD'S WILL

What if you could know God's will for your life—from beginning to end? What if you could know in advance the best school to attend, or the right job to take, or the perfect person to marry? Life would be so much easier, right? Not necessarily. In fact, knowing in advance—and in every detail—what God wants you to do might just scare you to death!

You would know about all this great stuff God has in mind for you, and it might seem incredible. Or you would know about the tough times God will allow you to go through, and it might seem impossible. Either way, you might forget that God delights in doing the incredible, and you might not remember that He has promised to get you through the impossible—leading you to play it safe the rest of your life.

Of course, that's not what God wants for you. He doesn't want you to play it safe. God wants more for you than you could possibly want for yourself:

> *"No eye has seen, no ear has heard, and no mind has imagined what God has prepared for those who love him."*
>
> 1 CORINTHIANS 2:9 NLT

Even though you don't know exactly what God has prepared for you, you can be sure He has your best interest in mind. Meanwhile, you don't have to be completely in the dark when it comes to knowing God's will. And that means you can trust Him in good times and bad, when you're rich and when you're poor, when you're healthy and when you're sick. God doesn't change just because your circumstances do.

Never forget that God knows you better than you know yourself, and He knows what's best for you. God knows your weaknesses, and He knows your strengths. God knows your fears, and He knows your hopes. God will never mislead you or do you harm.

> *"For I know the plans I have for you," says the LORD. "They are plans for good and not for disaster, to give you a future and a hope."*
>
> JEREMIAH 29:11 NLT

Try to see things from God's perspective. When you insist on seeing God's will from *your* perspective, then your main concern is *doing* stuff for God. You get caught up in your own performance. By contrast, when you see God's will from His perspective, you are more concerned about *being*. Sure, God wants you to do stuff for Him, but He's more interested in the kind of person you are *becoming* than the specific things you are *doing*. He knows that when your *being* is right, your *doing* will be right, and you will be doing more things that please Him.

Commit yourself to the will of God. This means trusting that God has your best interests in mind at all times. Trusting God for your future—whether that future is tomorrow or ten years from now—begins with trusting God *now*. Once you have committed to doing God's will—regardless of what it is and what it costs—God will guide you every step of the way.

> *Trust in the LORD with all your heart; do not depend on your own understanding. Seek his will in all you do, and he will direct your paths.*
>
> PROVERBS 3:5–6

. . .IN THE SMALL STUFF

- The best thing about God's will is that it is always the best.
- God doesn't love you for what you do; He loves you for who you are.
- That being said, God loves it when you do what He wants you to do.

"This son of mine was dead and has now returned to life. He was lost, but now he is found."
LUKE 15:24 NLT

= 79 =

WHEN CHILDREN TURN AWAY

There are those children every parent dreams of having: they are respectful, loving, successful, and ambitious. Then there are those children parents actually have: disrespectful, petulant, stubborn, and lazy. You may not be a parent, but trust us—having kids is no picnic. Sure, parenthood has its share of thrills and unexpected joy, but it can also include overwhelming heartache and sorrow.

Thankfully, most kids grow out of those periods of rebellion that seem to foam and fester during the teenage years, paving the way for those glory years when, as adult children, they establish satisfying and meaningful relationships with their parents (and may even deliver a parent's greatest joy—grandchildren!). But there are situations in some families when it seems as though a wayward child will never return. Maybe that's where you are right now. Perhaps you are the parent of a child who has turned away and shows no signs of turning back.

You have done all you can, and yet it never seems enough. Some days you weep for your child, and other days anger fills your eyes with tears. Can you handle any more grief? Will things ever change? Is there any hope?

The short answer for all three of these questions is *yes.* You can handle it, things will change, and there is hope. How do we know? God has promised it. Whether you're dealing with a wayward child or some other heartbreaking situation, God has promised to see you through.

> *No test or temptation that comes your way is beyond the course of what others have had to face. All you need to remember is that God will never let you down; he'll never let you be pushed past your limit; he'll always be there to help you come through it.*
>
> 1 CORINTHIANS 10:13 MSG

No matter how dark the night, there is always the dawn. No matter how strong the storm, there will always be a calm. Things will change. That's not to say that your wayward child will change. There's no guarantee of that, because your children, despite your best efforts, must make their own choices and accept responsibility for them. Your child may not have a change of heart, but the experience will change yours.

At the same time, no matter how long you wait for

things to turn around, always hold out hope. Remember the story of the prodigal son? Jesus told this parable, found in Luke 15:11–32, to remind us never to give up on those who stray. After demanding and then losing his inheritance, the younger son in the parable returned home to ask forgiveness for his many indiscretions. Rather than reprimand his son or tell him, "It's about time you came crawling back," the father rejoiced and embraced his lost son, throwing a great banquet in his honor.

Where did this attitude come from? It came from a heart of love and compassion, from someone who never gave up on his son. If you need an example of someone who has this heart, you need only think of your heavenly Father, who has never stopped loving you and has never given up on you.

"I have loved you, my people, with an everlasting love. With unfailing love I have drawn you to myself."

JEREMIAH 31:3 NLT

. . . IN THE SMALL STUFF

- Children bring us happiness and children bring us grief. Either way, they bring us tears.

- Hope doesn't come from what you can do. Hope comes from what God can do.

- Knowing that God won't give up on you keeps you from giving up on others.

*Growing old is like being increasingly
penalized for a crime you haven't committed.*
ANTHONY POWELL

CARING FOR AGING PARENTS

Sociologists have a term for them: the "Hinge Generation." These are the adults who simultaneously have
responsibility for their minor children and for their aged
parents. It's a relatively new generational demographic that
occurs because married couples are having children at a
later age and advances in health care allow people to live
longer. Instead of an average life expectancy in the upper
sixties, it is now more common for people to live into their
seventies, eighties, and even nineties.

While the increase in life expectancy is a wonderful
thing, it is accompanied by challenges to traditional family dynamics. There are unspoken—and often misunder-
stood—tensions that develop. The logistics of caring for an
aging parent often create mounting frustrations for each
generation. Both feel imposed upon.

It is easy for children to harbor resentment for the care they are required to render to their parents. They quite understandably feel:

- A loss of freedom. They already have a hectic schedule and a calendar full of commitments: taking care of their children, managing a home, pressures on the job, and social obligations. What little free time they once had must now be allocated to caring for a parent. While they might never refer to it as a "burden," it is certainly an obligation that is disruptive to their family life and previous routine.

- A loss of context. These adult children suffer a loss that relates to their station in life. Up until this point, they have always been able to seek wisdom and comfort from their parents. But they are now deprived of parental guidance due perhaps to Alzheimer's disease or the introspection and self-centeredness that often accompanies old age. Although they have a parent who is still living, they have no one who assumes the parental role in their lives. The declining capacities of the parents have effectively left these children as orphans. They must mourn the loss of a parental figure in their lives while still attending to the needs of their parents.

But these children must also realize that their parents have undergone some drastic changes in their circumstances, too; many times it is not a change of their choosing, being forced upon them by declining health. Their physical limitations and diminishing mental acuity can result in a significant restriction of the activities they previously enjoyed. Despite the efforts of their adult children to provide appropriate living arrangements, the older generation feels:

- A loss of independence. Their lives are suddenly defined more by the things they can't do than by the things that they are able to do. They may be told when to eat and what to eat. They may have lost their mobility, either by being deprived of driving privileges or by being confined to a wheelchair or forced to use a walker. They may not even be allowed to handle their own finances.

- A loss of dignity. They are well aware of the fact that their loss of freedom places them in a circumstance somewhat similar to a small child. Their own children are now their care providers—in a classic role reversal, the parent has become the child. While this is a part of a natural progression, it is nonetheless humiliating. These once proud and independent people are now living under stringent rules and regulations that clearly imply they can't be trusted to make decisions for themselves.

This sociological phenomenon has not caught God off guard. The advances in medical science that contributed to these circumstances do not surprise Him. He is not powerless to bring strength and love into these difficult situations.

Remember that God is the grand designer of the family. The family unit is so sacred that He uses it to describe His relationship with us. (He is our heavenly Father and we are His children.) Before the creation of the universe

He knew that the twenty-first century would find adult children caring for their parents. This is a circumstance that is clearly within His plan, so He will certainly make His spiritual strength available to those who are in it.

- God honors the love that is shown among family members.
- Care for your aged parents with the same love and mercy God has shown to you.
- Treat your parents in their old age in the manner that you hope to be treated by your own children.

We will never forget them, nor the last time
we saw them. . .as they prepared for their long
journey and waved good-bye and slipped the
surly bonds of Earth to touch the face of God.
RONALD REAGAN

= 81 =

THE LONG GOOD-BYE

Like a black cloud hovering on the horizon, the spec-ter of Alzheimer's disease looms. Already five million people in the United States and thirty million worldwide are afflicted with dementia in its most common forms—Alzheimer's disease and vascular dementia—impacting the lives of tens of millions more in the immediate circles of family and friends.

Those numbers are expected to grow dramatically as our population ages. About one in ten people over sixty-five, and as many as half of all people over the age of eighty-five, have Alzheimer's. It is now the eighth leading cause of death for people aged sixty-five and older. Health care costs are estimated to be more than fifty billion dollars per year.

It's not just the costly and deadly nature of this insidious condition that is most troubling. The personal impact of dementia and Alzheimer's, which Nancy Reagan called "the long good-bye," exacts the greatest toll. This is an illness that makes it hard for people to remember, think, and speak. It can make them seem moody or act strangely. The strong and vibrant man or woman you once knew as a husband or wife, mom or dad, grandfather or grandmother, uncle, aunt, or friend changes in ways that are subtle at first and then dramatic. On the outside they look normal, but on the inside things are clearly different. There seems to be an emptiness, a loss of personal identity. Dementia is the slow death of the brain, and as yet the cause cannot be entirely explained. Nor is there an entirely effective treatment or a cure.

But there is hope! Dr. Walt Russell, New Testament professor at Talbot School of Theology and a good friend, knows that now. Seventeen years ago he came face-to-face with the reality of dementia in his own mother. For seventeen years he watched her slide "more and more deeply into its abyss." For Walt, dementia isn't just a faceless statistic. It has his mother's face.

Just before his mother died, Walt felt compelled to write her a letter, reflecting on her life and the way he had been dealing with her condition. The letter led Walt to wrestle with some of the hard questions surrounding dementia. Because Walt's mother was a long-time Christian, many of these questions took on a spiritual nature:

- What became of her relationship with God when she lost most of her ability to think and reason?

- Did she continue to enjoy God's loving care and the presence of the Holy Spirit?

- Did God continue to care for her, Spirit-to-spirit, in spite of those damaged brain cells?

- Did she experience, in the depths of her soul, the promise of Jesus never to leave or forsake her?

- Did her soul still have the capacity to will—to choose to trust God—in spite of her dementia?

As Walt wrestled with these questions and the larger issues surrounding them, he came to a place where he believed his mother would have answered "yes" to all his questions. "My sense is that *her inability* to express an awareness of God's tender presence with her had no effect on *His ability* to be with her in the struggle. My hope and prayer is that she was never really alone in her dementia all those years."

If you are struggling with a family member or friend with dementia, may this be your hope. And may you offer this hope to others caught up in the struggle.

> *That is why we never give up. Though our bodies are dying, our spirits are being renewed every day.*
>
> 2 CORINTHIANS 4:16 NLT

- Even though a person cannot think, it doesn't mean he or she cannot feel.

- The value of life should never be determined by the quality of life.

- When Jesus said He would never leave us nor forsake us, He meant it.

There is only one class in the community that thinks more about money than the rich, and that is the poor. The poor can think of nothing else. That is the misery of being poor.
Oscar Wilde

= 82 =

FROM BUSTED TO BELIEF

There are times when you realize that, while life is tough, it could get worse. That can be a sobering prospect, but you might find comfort in the fact that you aren't as low as you could be:

- Illness is bad, but at least you aren't dead.

- Being underemployed is bad, but being unemployed would be worse.

- Loneliness is bad, but at least you're not hated by everyone you know.

- Being in debt is bad, but you're not in a debtor's prison.

Actually, debtors' prisons were closed more than one hundred years ago. So now when you hit bottom financially, bankruptcy is as bad as it gets. But that's bad—you can't get any lower. Unlike being in debt (which can keep accumulating), bankruptcy is the financial equivalent of waving the white flag. You give up. You concede. You are defeated. You're basically saying, "Come and take everything I've got."

In most respects, total financial failure is a bad place to be. But from a spiritual perspective, it's also a place where you can begin to deepen your relationship with God. Perhaps God considers it necessary to bring you to a place of complete financial brokenness so you can understand that *God is all I've got.*

When you've had everything taken from you, one thing is painfully obvious: all you have is God. When your cars are repossessed, you still have God. When the bank has foreclosed on your home, you still have God. When your savings are depleted and the cupboards are bare, you still have God. When you have lost all your worldly possessions, you still have God. He will never leave you or forget you. He is your one and only constant in life. Let the fact of His eternal presence be a comfort to you. You are never without anything because you always have God.

But understanding that God is all you have is just the first step. As you deepen your relationship with God, you can discover that *God is all I need.*

Living at the lowest rung of the financial ladder can teach you that so much of our material world is superfluous. At the most elementary level, very few things are necessities of life. Because God has promised to provide everything we *need*, He is all we need. He'll make sure we have the basics (although He is likely to expect we'll be contributing effort and energy). Once the basics are covered, we can truly enjoy the non-material blessings that God offers (love, joy, peace, etc.).

But it doesn't stop at that point. There is one further step in the process of maturing in your faith. Once you understand that God is the source of everything you need, the material objects of life become distractions. Recognizing that God is the sole source of everything that really matters, you may suddenly come to the liberating realization that *God is all I want.*

Now you've reached the depth of spiritual maturity that God desires for you. When you aren't worried about what you *have*, and when you aren't distracted by what you *need*, you are free from the entanglements that accompany financial worries. You realize that material possessions have absolutely no significance when compared to the privilege of having a personal acquaintanceship with God. If the things that money can buy divert your attention from God, then you don't want them. Whether you have wealth or not becomes irrelevant so long as you can have God.

Is this last stage of spiritual maturity unrealistic? Is it purely theoretical and impossible to reach? It may seem so, but that is only because we have not broken free from the grip of materialism. For the apostle Paul—who had experienced both a life of privilege and a life of poverty—his financial status was irrelevant:

I have learned how to get along happily whether I have much or little. I know how to live on almost nothing or with everything. I have learned the secret of living in every situation, whether it is with a full stomach or empty, with plenty or little.

PHILIPPIANS 4:11–12

What was Paul's secret? Realizing that God was all he had, all he needed, and all he wanted. Make that secret yours.

. . . IN THE SMALL STUFF

- You'll enjoy life more if you value the quality of relationships more than the quantity of possessions.

- Going without can be a good thing if it causes you to go with God.

- Sometimes you have to look past the possessions to discover God's presence.

Work is an extension of personality.
It is achievement. It is one of the ways
in which a person defines himself,
measures his worth and his humanity.
PETER F. DRUCKER

= 83 =

A LOSS OF SELF

Sometimes events and circumstances—such as illness, financial struggles, or broken relationships—are what make you feel like you are experiencing tough times. But sometimes your difficulties are the result of unfulfilled expectations. This occurs when your life isn't really bad, but something less than you wanted it to be. In comparison to your friends, your circumstance may not be difficult—but it can be very depressing stacked up against what you have been desperately hoping for.

Your unmet expectations can take many forms:

- You lost your job.
- You didn't get promoted.
- You've been demoted.
- You haven't attained the financial security you expected.
- You're in a dead-end job you hate.
- You never obtained that educational degree.

Disappointments, if not dealt with, can gnaw away at you. The disappointment over unmet expectations evolves into disappointment with yourself. There is an insidious shift in your unhappiness. It moves from dejection over *what* you have failed to achieve and turns into a disappointment over *who* you are:

- I lost my job, so I'm an incompetent person.
- I never completed any degree, so I lack ambition.
- I didn't get the promotion, so I'm a loser.
- I'm financially insecure, so I'm a big failure.

Don't fall into the trap of defining yourself by what you have accomplished—or failed to. Your sense of self should be determined by your character traits (integrity, friendliness, loyalty, responsibility, etc.), not by the achievements on your résumé.

In case you doubt a change of perspective will ease the pain of an unmet expectation, take the "Eulogy Quiz."

Don't worry; there is only one question:

> When the eulogy is given at your funeral, would you rather have your life evaluated by
> A. the status of your achievements; or
> B. the lives that were positively impacted by your character?

Few people would choose option A. Achievements quickly become empty and meaningless when you have been placed six feet below the earth's surface. On the other hand, kindness and encouragement to others (option B) make a legacy that remains long after your death.

And remember this: You aren't the best judge of the significance of your unmet expectations. You're not objective. After all, you're likely to be tempted to attribute too much importance to the thing you have been hoping for. (People most often obsess over expectations that will make their lives easier or make them appear successful to others—things related to prestige, status, or wealth. People very seldom evaluate themselves according to the more substantive and internal character qualities of life—things that aren't as readily apparent to others.)

Why not turn the matter of your unmet expectations over to God? If God thinks it is essential that you obtain what you have hoped for, He can work in the circumstances of your life to bring it about. But don't expect God to lose sleep over the job you lost or some other opportunity that passed you by. Of course those things are important to

Him (because they are important to you), but He is less concerned about your status and more concerned about the kind of person you are.

In God's paradigm, you are not evaluated by what you have failed to achieve. He is more interested in the character you display in the face of your unmet expectations.

- Are you going to mope or are you going to become motivated?

- Are you going to be critically introspective, or will you look expectantly for what God has next?

- Are you going to spiral downward from disappointment to despair, or will you display the character of overcoming your failure?

God is the best career advisor you can find. Include Him in the evaluation process of determining what you should do and who you should become.

. . .IN THE SMALL STUFF

- The kind of person you are is a matter of your character, not your circumstances.

- An unmet expectation is the perfect occasion for meeting God.

- When people are fondly remembered, it is for the compassion in their hearts—not for the list of their accomplishments.

God has given us two hands—
one for receiving and the other for giving.
BILLY GRAHAM

= 84 =

GIVING TO GOD

Wherever your treasure is, there your heart and thoughts will also be." In that simple sentence, Jesus touched the center point of human nature when it comes to money and possessions. If we are storing up treasure in heaven, our hearts will follow after God and His eternal values. If our goal is to store up treasure on earth, our hearts will more often than not be bound by greed and insecurity, caught in the tension between always wanting more and never having enough.

Is your life characterized by one frustrating financial crisis after another? Is your mind preoccupied with money woes? Do you wish you could give to more worthy causes, but never seem to have enough left over at the end of the month? Then it's likely that you are attempting to store up your treasure on earth.

If that's the case, you aren't a bad person—and you certainly aren't alone. Many people who desire to follow God with all their heart struggle in this area. In fact, all believers—if they are being honest—have to fight the urge to build up earthly treasure. We are so concerned about making and protecting our money that we have a natural tendency to take our focus off heaven, where all we have comes from in the first place.

We may think we earn money and own things, but the reality is that everything we have comes from God. We aren't owners; we are stewards, entrusted by God to wisely manage the resources He has given us. Everything we have—money, possessions, even our abilities and talents—are gifts from God. Of course, God wants us to enjoy what He has given us, but He also wants us to acknowledge His ownership by giving it back to Him. In fact, God promises to bless us if we do! By contrast, He will withhold His blessing if we don't.

So how do we give back to God? We can't suddenly give Him money we don't have. It starts small, with little amounts of our money and time, given to God with open hands. And it takes thought and prayer. You need to carefully consider what God wants you to do. In time, God will show you some specific opportunities, and you will build up your ability to give to God. Then, as you do, your heart will be blessed, and you will find yourself wanting to give more. That's just the way it works.

If you are wondering where you should begin giving to God, you can start by giving generously to others. An altruistic and willing heart pleases God because it takes your eyes off yourself and puts them on the people around you. "For God loves the person who gives cheerfully" (2 Corinthians 9:7 NLT).

Here's something else about giving to God. When you give generously and cheerfully to others—whether it's to your church, a charitable organization, or individuals serving Christ in ministry—you don't have to worry about your own needs, because God will be generous to you. "Then you will always have everything you need and plenty left over to share with others" (2 Corinthians 9:8 NLT).

Another principle to follow in your giving is to help the poor. As the scriptures say,

"Godly people give generously to the poor.
Their good deeds will never be forgotten."
2 CORINTHIANS 9:9 NLT

Even more, "Whoever gives to the poor will lack nothing. But a curse will come upon those who close their eyes to poverty" (Proverbs 28:27 NLT).

Do you see the pattern here? God promises to bless those who store their treasure in heaven by being generous to others—in particular, the poor. People who insist on hoarding treasure on earth will not experience God's blessing. But don't just be generous for generosity's sake. Guard your heart. Make sure you are giving in order to gain God's approval, not to impress others or to quietly congratulate yourself. Giving to God means just that—giving Him all you have so you will become all that He wants you to be.

- If you never have enough at the end of the month, perhaps you aren't giving God enough at the beginning.

- It's not the size of the check that counts; it's the condition of the heart.

- God doesn't need your money, but He knows you need to give your money.

Illness is a convent which has its rule,
its austerity, its silences, and its inspirations.
ALBERT CAMUS

= 85 =

CONFRONTED WITH CANCER

Cancer—the word nobody likes to hear. From a technical standpoint, cancer is a change in the normal growth of cells, causing them to spread and destroy healthy tissues and organs of the body. But from an emotional perspective, cancer is one of the most devastating pronouncements a person and his or her family can receive. It's not exactly a death sentence, but that's the first thing many people think when a medical professional gives them the news.

Thanks to advances in research and development, many types of cancer that were virtually incurable several years ago are now very treatable—if caught early enough. So there is reason for hope. Still, cancer can be devastating to a family. If you, a member of your family, or a close friend is suffering from cancer right now, you understand what we're talking about. It isn't easy to confront, and it can't always be beaten. But it doesn't have to get the best of you.

You learn a lot about people when they come face-to-face with the life-and-death ping-pong struggle of a dreaded disease. Over the last few years we've watched a half-dozen family members and close friends battle cancer. Although each one had a different form of the disease, they shared much in common—primarily the fact that all were people of faith. It didn't matter whether they had a modest or vital relationship with God when they first received their diagnosis. As their treatment—and in some cases, the disease—progressed, so did their connection with God. Though they suffered from the physical effects of the disease and the potency of the treatment, the immaterial part of their being gained strength.

> *That is why we never give up. Though our bodies are dying, our spirits are being renewed every day.*
> 2 CORINTHIANS 4:16 NLT

One friend who had always been a driven, successful businessman fought valiantly against a brain tumor. When his cancer prevented him from working daily, he took calls at home, mostly to encourage his coworkers. In the final few months, colleagues, friends, and family came to his side—at home or in the hospital. They came to offer the few words of encouragement they could muster, and invariably, they left feeling as though *they* were the ones who had been blessed.

A family member with a cancer that responded successfully to treatment began sending e-mails to a network of people who had committed to pray for him. Those of us who received his messages looked forward to reading them, filled as they were with praise to God.

> For our present troubles are quite small and won't last very long. Yet they produce for us an immeasurably great glory that will last forever!
>
> 2 Corinthians 4:17 nlt

A friend who struggled with breast cancer was tireless in her efforts to find the best doctors and course of treatment. Like so many cancer patients, her family gave her incredible support. When she lost her hair due to chemotherapy, her husband told everyone she was more beautiful than ever. He set up a prayer network and reported specific needs so we could all pray.

Regardless of the outcomes, each one of our friends and family members who battled cancer gave us a glimpse of eternity. Some have passed on to the ultimate pain-free, disease-free, and stress-free life with God, while others are thanking their Creator for more years here on earth. For the latter, even in recovery, they seem to hold on to that connection to the eternal, knowing that for all of us, it's just a matter of time before we experience what God has prepared for those who love Him.

> So we don't look at the troubles we can see right now; rather, we look forward to what we have not yet seen. For the troubles we see will soon be over, but the joys to come will last forever.
>
> 2 Corinthians 4:18 nlt

- Only those who have had cancer understand that even a deadly disease can bring blessings.

- The condition of the body has little or no relationship to the condition of the spirit.

- The best thing you can do for someone experiencing the tough times of cancer is to offer encouragement and prayer.

The whole point of this life is the healing of the heart's eye through which God is seen.
SAINT AUGUSTINE

= 86 =

DOES GOD STILL HEAL?

While He lived on this earth, Jesus Christ was known for many things. He was a spellbinding teacher, He performed wondrous miracles, and He spoke many dramatic prophecies. As He traveled throughout His home region of Galilee, Jesus also "healed people who had every kind of sickness and disease" (Matthew 4:23 NLT). Healing was an important part of the ministry of Jesus. Beyond simply curing the diseases and deformities of people, the miraculous healings of Jesus authenticated His divine nature.

When Jesus healed—like the time He opened the ears and loosed the tongue of a man born deaf and mute—the large crowd that followed Him was amazed. Again and again the people said, "Everything he does is wonderful" (Mark 7:37 NLT). Eventually, the people became preoccupied with

Christ's healing power. Whenever He entered a region, the word would spread and the sick would come, desperate for a healing touch.

It's no different today. There's not a sick person who doesn't desire healing. Most people rely on the expertise and care of medical doctors, whose expert diagnoses, correct prescriptions, and gifted hands often bring wholeness to our wounded bodies, emotions, and minds. Other people go directly to God—or to a minister of God—and ask for miraculous healing. No doubt you've seen the parades of people on television shows putting their hope in so-called faith healers. Perhaps you have attended such a meeting with the hope that God would heal you.

Does God still heal? Jesus isn't here among us physically to perform His miracles, but He is with us spiritually—and He is certainly capable of healing bodies, minds, and emotions. After all, He made them!

If God still heals, does He use the skills of the medical community exclusively, or does He work through the promises of faith healers? Or does God utilize a variety of methods?

To get to the heart of healing, we need to go back to Jesus. Yes, physical healing was an important part of His earthly ministry, but Jesus had more than the *physical* in mind when He healed people.

> *"Healthy people don't need a doctor—sick people do. I have come to call sinners, not those who think they are already good enough."*
>
> MARK 2:17 NLT

Jesus was the Great Physician because He healed both physical and *spiritual* sickness. The good news for us is that Jesus still does that today. There is no sickness or sin problem He can't handle.

> *Praise the LORD, I tell myself, and never forget the good things he does for me. He forgives all my sins and heals all my diseases.*
>
> PSALM 103:2–3 NLT

When we or someone we love is facing an illness, we need to remember that the most important healing touch anyone can receive is spiritual. Whenever Jesus healed, that was always His first concern. In fact, focusing too much on the physical can distract us from the most important issue—our spiritual condition. Yes, God still heals physically, but that's not His primary concern. Because we will be completely healed in heaven, God's bigger concern is that we get there.

. . .IN THE SMALL STUFF

- No doctor is a god, but God can use doctors to accomplish His purposes.
- The person who doesn't think God can heal doesn't think much of God.
- If you always keep heaven in mind, you will think less about healing and more about the Healer.

Everyone has noticed how hard it is to turn our thoughts to God when everything is going well with us. We "have all we want" is a terrible saying when "all" does not include God.
C. S. Lewis

= 87 =

HEARING GOD

One of the great lies of humanism is that all suffering is bad. The skeptic—that is, the one who doubts that God exists—argues that suffering demonstrates there is no all-good and all-powerful God in charge of this world. If there were such a God, the skeptic says, He would not allow suffering of any kind.

The problem with this argument is that in the practical world of human experience (as opposed to the theoretical world of academic reasoning), we know better. While no one looks forward to pain and suffering, and no one wants to see it inflicted on others, there is no denying that suffering can be helpful. Indeed, you could say that rather than separating us from God, suffering does a pretty good job of pointing us toward Him.

In a perfect world, of course, suffering doesn't belong. God created this world to be perfect, and there was no such thing as suffering. After He finished His creation, God pronounced it "good." Then sin entered the world, marring the goodness. It wasn't that God had lost control or interest in His world. Sin was allowed to enter because He created us with the capacity to freely choose (or reject) Him. The effect of sin was dramatic, for with it came physical and spiritual death. But there was yet another consequence. In the words of Peter Kreeft, sin "made us stupid, so that we can only learn the hard way."

It would be great if, in our present state, we could follow God and learn wisdom and virtue in a pain-free environment. But the fact of the matter is that we are fallen creatures—and most of the time we are drawn to God only when things aren't going well. In his book *The Problem of Pain*, C. S. Lewis addresses this idea head-on. He refers to pain as "God's megaphone," serving the purpose of getting our attention. He writes:

> *No doubt Pain as God's megaphone is a terrible instrument; it may lead to final and unrepented rebellion. But it gives the only opportunity the bad man can have for amendment. It removes the veil; it plants the flag of truth within the fortress of a rebel soul.*

Have you found that true in your own life? Did you first surrender to God because your life was in great shape or because you were in the midst of crisis? Are you drawn closer to God now when things go well or when you experience difficulties? It's easy to put God off when things are going well, because who really needs Him then? As Saint Augustine said, "God wants to give us something, but cannot, because our hands are full—there's nowhere for Him to put it."

Truth is, when we experience pain and suffering, we are much more in tune to God—not because God enjoys our trials, but because He delights in getting us through them. Not only can we hear God's voice more clearly through our pain, but we long to hear Him. What does He want from us? What does He have for us? How about courage and strength? How about truth and wisdom? How about patience and a clearer understanding of the way things really are in the world? As Kreeft writes, "It seems that everything that has intrinsic value, everything that cannot be bought or negotiated, or compromised or relativized or reduced, goes with suffering."

Unless you make it a point to hear God, the hard stuff in your life will seem random and meaningless. On the other hand, when you seek God and listen to His voice, your present troubles will draw you closer to Him. There, safe in His arms, you may not get all the answers you're looking for—but you will find meaning in the midst of your pain.

- In the midst of your pain, opening your ears to God will automatically open your heart.

- Our suffering matters to God. It matters so much that He subjected His own Son to the worst kind.

- If you can't hear God in the tough times of your life, it's unlikely you will hear Him in the good times.

Jesus loves the little children,
All the children of the world.
Red and yellow, black and white,
They are precious in His sight;
Jesus loves the little children of the world.
CHILDREN'S CHORUS

= 88 =

WHEN CHILDREN SUFFER

Of all the tough times we experience or observe in the world, the most incomprehensible is the suffering of children.

If it's your own child hurting, you will do anything to ease the pain. A father was holding his newborn baby when someone asked, "Would you throw yourself in front of a car to save him?" Without hesitation he replied, "Absolutely!" Although the father had known his child for just a few days, the bond was permanently set. We will do anything to protect our children and to keep them from harm.

Even when we observe the suffering of other children—the poor and starving in Africa or young ones afflicted with disease in our own land—our hearts melt. What can be done? Who'll stop their pain?

Much is being done to bring relief to these little ones. If we are so inclined, we can join the heroic efforts of organizations such as World Vision and Compassion International, who help millions of children around the globe every day. It's not unusual for a church to sponsor hundreds of orphaned children from a single village, where hunger and disease have devastated the adult population. Where they once fought a daily battle for survival, these children now have food, clothing, shelter, an education—and hope. Hundreds of children out of millions who are suffering may seem like a drop in the proverbial bucket, but it is a start.

On our own continent, we may not see suffering on the same scale, but our hearts break for little ones whose bodies are ravaged by cancer and other cruel diseases. Maybe you are experiencing something like that in your own family, or perhaps you know someone whose child is fighting for his or her life. It's a hard thing to watch because the children seem so helpless. Yet we must not give up hope, for just when we wonder if anything can be done for these kids, we see the outstanding and tireless work of research organizations, such as the Muscular Dystrophy Association, in seeking a cure for these childhood maladies.

Mattie Stepanek, the bright-eyed boy with muscular dystrophy who died weeks before his fourteenth birthday, became an eloquent advocate for all hurting children when he began writing to cope with his own struggle. His stirring poems, prayers, essays, and stories on topics like grief, love, disability, and peace became anthems for a world touched by the resilience of one whose physical condition never dimmed his spirit. Who can forget his bright eyes and knowing smile, especially when he recited one of his touching poems, which he called "heartsongs"?

We may hurt over the pain the children of the world experience, but we must never forget that God holds them in His hand. When Jesus walked the earth, He invited the children to come to Him, even when it wasn't convenient, or when bigger issues seemed to press upon Him. Once some parents brought their children to Jesus so He could touch them and bless them, but His disciples didn't think He had time for the little ones. Jesus reprimanded them by saying,

> *"Let the children come to me. Don't stop them! For the Kingdom of God belongs to such as these. I assure you, anyone who doesn't have their kind of faith will never get into the Kingdom of God."*
> MARK 10:14–15 NLT

Then Jesus picked up the children, held them in His arms, and blessed them by placing His hands on their heads. That's how much He loves the children, all the children of the world.

Despite our best efforts to provide relief and to help find a cure for those children who are hurting and who need a healing touch—and these efforts should never stop—we must remember that God's mercy and grace never go away, and sometimes they shine brightest through the weakest of vessels. The lessons we learn from all children, especially those who are suffering, should make us better people and our world a better place.

. . .IN THE SMALL STUFF

- The tears of a hurting child should bring us to tears.
- Don't let the needs of the world overwhelm you— let them motivate you.
- Teach your own children about the needs of other children. You will be surprised at how much they can do.

It is one of the mysteries of our nature that man, all unprepared, can receive a thunder stroke [of bad news] and live. There is but one reasonable explanation of it. The intellect is stunned by the shock and but gropingly gathers the meaning of the words. The power to realize their full import is mercifully lacking.

<small>MARK TWAIN, ON RECEIVING NEWS OF THE DEATH OF A LOVED ONE</small>

= 89 =

GOING FROM HURTING TO HEALING

Writing this book focused our thoughts on the many tragedies that occur in life. Each one is different and—for the lives affected—very personal. While we would never attempt to prioritize tough times according to severity, we are struck by the disruption caused by an unexpected death. Whether caused by an unpredicted heart attack, a car accident, or murder, the death of a loved one leaves you hanging...without warning, so many things are left unsaid. There's not even a chance to say a simple good-bye.

It occurred to us that someone with particular insights on premature death might be the county coroner. The occasion of our visit occurred on the one-year anniversary of a multiple murder investigated by her and the rest of the coroner's staff. In a tragedy defying imagination, nine related women and children, living in a single household, had been shot to death.

We wondered how a professional investigator deals with the abject horror of such a situation. Does she become calloused and insensitive over time? Can she remove the thoughts from her mind when she returns home? Is she ever able to shake the specter of death? She answered all of our questions by stating the philosophy of her office: on the technical side, it is the coroner's job to determine the cause of death; but on the human and emotional side, it is the role of her office to help survivors deal with their loss. She concluded her comments to us by saying, "We try to make a good thing out of a bad thing."

The lesson we learned from the county coroner may help you deal with catastrophes that happen in your world. Her advice can apply whether you are directly affected by a tragedy within your family, or are the friend of a person impacted by a disastrous event. When misfortune strikes, look for an opportunity to make a positive difference in another person's life. Look for those who are hurting—even though you may be grieving yourself. Consider how the sadness of the situation can be alleviated—even just a bit—by some kindness on your part. Consider that your role in restoring these people involves moving them from a place of hurting to a place of healing.

This perspective is not limited to occurrences of death. It can apply to all the tough times in life. The misfortune that strikes someone's life could be physical, in many ways other than death—a chronic illness, a compulsive eating disorder, or a diagnosis of Alzheimer's disease. Or the adversity could be emotional—living in a difficult marriage, dealing with a rebellious child, or facing myriad other antagonistic relationships. Or the hardship could be financial—the loss of a job, a broken-down car without money to fix it, or the constant strain of debt with the accompanying worry that there won't be enough money for rent and groceries.

These are the situations happening all around you. And even if you find yourself in the middle of the storm, there are many others affected, too. So change your perspective. Don't focus on the tragedy; that will only make you morose. And don't think only about how you are impacted; that will make you self-centered. Look at the others who are hurting. Commit yourself to the noble effort of making a difference in their lives. Endeavor to make good out of a bad thing. Do whatever it takes to move them from a place of hurting to a place of healing. Don't assume that others will do it. Take on the responsibility yourself. The person you help will be better for what you have done. And so will you.

. . .In the Small Stuff

- Don't turn away from a tragedy. Consider it an opportunity to make a positive difference in someone's life.

- You can't stop tough times from happening. But you can work to achieve some good result in a bad situation.

- The best thing you can do for yourself in your grief is to help other people in theirs.

In that day the wolf and lamb will live togeth-
er; the leopard and the goat will be at peace.
Calves and yearlings will be safe among lions,
and a little child will lead them all.
ISAIAH 11:6 NLT

= 90 =

WILL YOUR PET BE IN HEAVEN?

One of the most beautiful pictures of God's glorious future kingdom—where there will be everlasting peace, beauty, and goodness—is the complete harmony among the animals. Here on earth, there is anything but harmony. Wild animals' interactions are generally "eat or be eaten." Even our domesticated animals don't always get along.

As for our relationship with the animals, it's not exactly ideal, either. Though God commanded us to care for the animals, we don't always do a very good job. Still, one of God's great blessings is the pleasure animals bring us. We enjoy their beauty and admire their ability to survive in the wild. And when we adopt an animal and care for it in our home, we literally consider that pet a part of the family.

When an animal suffers, we feel its pain—so much so that we have enacted laws to prevent cruelty to animals. And when we lose a pet, we are sometimes surprised at the emotions that well up inside. Which leads us to the big question: what happens to an animal when it dies?

As you could predict, there are differing views on this issue. One says that when an animal dies, it ceases to exist. There's no possibility of an afterlife for animals because animals do not have an eternal, spiritual nature. Proponents of this view emphasize the differences between animals and people; though God created all living things, only human beings were created in His image. Here's the way it happened:

> *Then God said, "Let us make people in our image, to be like ourselves. They will be masters over all life—the fish in the sea, the birds in the sky, and all the livestock, wild animals, and small animals."*
> GENESIS 1:26 NLT

Because we are made in God's image, we possess qualities that animals don't. For example, we have a moral code built inside, giving us the sense of right and wrong. Animals, on the other hand, function by instinct. Furthermore, we have the ability to learn, reason, and use language in ways that animals can't. And we have an immaterial, spiritual dimension that enables us to relate personally to God. We can pray to God, praise Him, and hear Him speak to us. No animal has ever had that ability.

It is this spiritual part of humankind that lasts forever. Though our bodies die, our spirits continue to exist. Without a spiritual dimension, some say, animals cannot live forever. When their bodies die, they simply cease to exist. The conclusion of this view is that there will be no animals in heaven, at least not the animals we have known on earth.

Of course, that isn't the only view. Another perspective presents a different picture. While agreeing that there is a spiritual difference between humans and animals, this view allows for the presence of animals in heaven. We see from scripture that animals will be part of God's kingdom on earth, so why couldn't they be in heaven? If there will be other nonhuman living things in heaven (such as green fields and flowers), why not animals?

But what about specific animals, such as your pet? The Bible doesn't speak to the question, so we can only speculate. Certainly, with God all things are possible. If He wanted to raise up your pet in the last days so that you might be reunited in heaven, He could. The focus of heaven will be our worship of Jesus Christ, the Lamb of God, but that doesn't necessarily exclude ordinary lambs or dogs or cats or other animals that could add to the supreme pleasure heaven promises.

In the meantime, we are to care for our animals just as we care for each other. This is what God does (see Psalm 36:6), and as creatures made in His image, we are to imitate Him in all we do.

- Animals were created for us to use—not misuse.

- Animals may not share certain capacities with us, such as the ability to reason, but there's one thing we do share: the capacity to suffer.

- Animals make us better humans.

It should be a pleasure to those that have their
home in the other world to think of being
"no more in this world"; for when we have done
what we have to do in this world. . .what is there
that should court our stay? When we receive a
sentence of death within ourselves, with a holy
triumph we should say. . ."now I shall wander no
more in this howling wilderness, be tossed no more
on this stormy sea; now I am no more in this world,
but can cheerfully quit it and give it a final farewell."
MATTHEW HENRY

= 91 =

AFRAID TO DEATH OF DYING

Woody Allen once said, "I'm not afraid of death. I just
don't want to be around when it happens." Most
of us feel the same way. Our own mortality is something
that we'd prefer not to confront. So we put off preparing a
will, and we don't talk with our families about funeral and
burial arrangements. Even when faced with terminal illness, many families discuss generic pleasantries and avoid

the emotional issues that accompany death. We simply do not want to think about what happens when we're gone.

But what are we so afraid of? Though it sounds ironic, death is a natural part of life. It will happen to everyone. It has already happened to people we know and love. Since it's so commonplace, why is there still such an apprehension of death?

Despite its pervasive presence in our world, death remains shrouded in mystery:

- For each of us, it is a first-time experience. Although others have gone through it, we haven't. Thus, we can't predict our feelings and emotional responses. Until it happens, we don't know how we will respond. Will we show bravery or cowardice?

- For most of us, we don't know the circumstances. Will our death be the result of an accident that ends our life quickly and unexpectedly? Or will our dying process be painful and prolonged due to a debilitating disease? Will we die with dignity or in circumstances we consider humiliating?

- For all of us, we have regrets. Because each of us is far from perfect, life is a trail of decisions, mistakes, and actions we would prefer to "do over." There are relationships that didn't end well, and goals left unaccomplished. We know that death not only terminates our life but also any possibility of concluding some of our unfinished business.

- For all of us, there are those we leave behind. It is not egotistical to acknowledge that family members and friends will mourn your death. Your quality relationship with them is revealed by your concern that they will experience sorrow at your passing. You don't want them to have to experience the grief associated with your death.

- For everyone else, life will go on. Although death brings finality to our lives, the rest of the world will continue living. This may cause us mixed emotions. We are glad for our survivors, but we realize that we are relatively dispensable in the large scheme of things. If life can go on without us, we question whether we were ever really needed.

It's no wonder that death causes apprehension if we focus myopically on all the unknowns. The negative symptoms of such a perspective can be reversed, however, if we approach death with our actual knowledge of life after death. For those who love God and have followed Him in life, death is the starting point of an eternal life characterized by:

- the presence of God Himself;
- the absence of evil;
- no pain and suffering;
- a whole and healthy spiritual body free of any defect or deformity;
- a reunion with others; and
- an eternal state of happiness, peace, and love.

Death is to be dreaded if we associate it only with the past and what is unknown. But death can be approached boldly and with anticipation if we view it in the context of our relationship with God. Our attitude about death is determined by our perspective: are we looking down at the world or up to heaven? This choice of perspective was articulated well by British theologian Austin Farrer:

> *When we [have died and are in heaven], and look back on earthly life, we shall not see it as a vigorous battlefield from which we have gracefully retired; we shall view it as an insubstantial dream from which we have happily awoken.*

When you are confronted with death, don't look back with regret or ahead with anxiety. Rejoice in the eternal life that awaits those who love God. According to His plan, your best is yet to come.

. . .In the Small Stuff

- You can't avoid death—but during this life you can make arrangements for how you will spend eternity.
- Considering the consequences of death may change your attitudes and actions in life.
- It may be inappropriate to wish for death, but everyone should long for heaven.

I know not what the future holds,
but I know who holds the future.
IRA F. STANPHILL

= 92 =

GOD IS IN THE SMALL STUFF
FOR TOUGH TIMES

Just saying the phrase *God is in the small stuff for tough times* doesn't make the tough times easier to endure. We are the first to admit that those six words are not a spiritual mantra that will make your difficult circumstances vanish—or even diminish. Just as saying "think thin and you'll be thin" will not shed unwanted pounds, neither will repeating the words "God is in the small stuff for tough times" relieve the pain and problems of your difficult circumstances.

We can imagine that these words are hollow to anyone in the midst of pain, suffering, and discouragement. Even the perspectives we have given in the preceding chapters may not seem immediately helpful. You might even wonder, *What good is God?* after reading the previous chapters:

- When we said God never intends to insulate you from problems, you may have heard: "God doesn't keep trouble from happening."

- When we said God can use difficult circumstances to make you a better person, you may have heard: "God won't make it hurt any less."

- And when we said God will be with you all the way until it ends, you may have thought: Yeah, but He doesn't make it end any quicker.

Sometimes the pain is so great you can't appreciate the long-range benefit of God's involvement. So let's deal with your very honest and understandable question: "What good is God?"

There is one immediate benefit to recognizing God is with you in the midst of your problems. It is what you need the most if you are going to hold up under the pressure of your adversity—peace.

Isn't that ironic? God promises to deliver the emotion that is completely contrary to the reaction the circumstances cause:

- When you feel pain—God promises peace.

- When you are living in fear—God promises peace.

- When you have unbearable stress—God promises peace.

- When you are brokenhearted with grief—God promises peace.

- When you are depressed and discouraged—God promises peace.

It just doesn't make sense, does it? How is peace possible in circumstances characterized by death, pain, danger, fear, and loss? Humanly speaking, peace is impossible in such situations. But with God, we aren't talking about *human* peace. We are dealing with a supernatural peace that is experienced only through knowing God. Here is how the Bible describes it:

> *Don't worry about anything; instead, pray about everything. Tell God what you need, and thank him for all he has done. If you do this, you will experience God's peace, which is far more wonderful than the human mind can understand. His peace will guard your hearts and minds as you live in Christ Jesus.*
> PHILIPPIANS 4:6–7 NLT

We won't attempt to define this kind of peace. As the Bible says, it is spiritually understood in the midst of your struggles. This peace—which surpasses our human understanding—doesn't make the problems go away. That's precisely why we need to experience it during those tough times. And this supernatural peace will not always make things easier in the ways you might hope:

- It won't repair a broken marriage.
- It won't cure the cancer.
- It won't replenish the bank account.
- It won't bring anyone back from the dead.

But it will make life better in ways that you can't imagine:

- You will feel God's presence.
- You will begin to see with God's perspective.
- You will hear God's voice.
- You will sense God's love.

And these things—despite the surrounding problems and suffering—will make life good.

. . .IN THE SMALL STUFF

- God's peace doesn't remove us from the world, but it makes living in the world possible.
- With God in the tough times, His peace is there, too.
- God doesn't offer us a life filled with peaceful pursuits. But He offers a peaceful life in a difficult world.

—from—

God Is in the Small Stuff at Christmas

Christmas is a time when people of all
religions come together to worship Jesus Christ.

Matt Groening (creator of *The Simpsons*)

= 93 =

GOD'S STORY

There are so many mental pictures associated with Christmas. Whether you're in snow-covered Vermont or sweltering Palm Springs, the word *Christmas* brings to mind images of:

- a decorated tree in your family room;

- that elaborate dinner set on a festive table surrounded by family members (both the normal and the abnormal);

- holiday shopping;

- the anticipation of opening Christmas cards from long-ago friends;

- the stockings hung on the mantel (which are purely decorative since people have stopped giving oranges as Christmas gifts); and

- brightly wrapped gifts under the tree.

Oh yes, and let's not forget the nativity scene.

For various reasons—apathy, vandalism, or efforts by the ACLU—you may not see a life-sized nativity in your town. But you might have a miniature version of the crèche prominently displayed in your home during the yuletide season. A little manger, holding a removable Baby Jesus, is always in the center; then you put Mary, seated on a hay bale, beside the manger; the kneeling Joseph is placed on the other side. Surrounding them is a wobbly stable that would probably fall over had you not strategically placed a sheep and donkey to prop it up. Also nearby are a few shepherd boys in various poses.

If you purchased the deluxe nativity kit, you also have a majestic angel with a six-inch wingspan. Since he's too heavy to place on top of the stable, you've got him taped to the wall. And the wise men, with camel, are also in the vicinity. (If you're a stickler for historical accuracy and know that the magi didn't visit Jesus until He was about two years old, you've placed the wise men, with camel, on the coffee table at the other end of the family room. That denotes their geographic distance from the manger on the night of Christ's birth.)

With the commercialization of Christmas, retailers are constantly providing a parade of paraphernalia to catch your imagination as the premier decoration for the holiday season. By its nature, the nativity scene is humble and unassuming, so it often loses out to other ornamentation with more flash and pizzazz. The status of that manger set in many homes might even be classified as "small stuff" at Christmastime.

Although it may be modest and unpretentious, the nativity scene presents the best image of Christmas. Unlike any other ornament or decoration, the manger setting—in its singular representation—conveys the essence of Christmas: that God loved the world so much that He was willing to send His Son to earth.

As you walk past the manger display in your living room, don't be so preoccupied that you miss the significance of what it stands for. There is a great "back story" behind that collection of figurines. Don't just think of Baby Jesus in a hay trough; realize that this was the Son of God who for eternity past had reigned in heaven. Imagine the celestial demotion of moving from heaven to earth, and don't overlook the indignity (and humiliation) of what He suffered when He assumed human form. (We might not consider taking on "human form" to be a cause of mortification, but it is if you are deity.)

Despite its comparatively bland appearance, the nativity scene is the premier Christmas decoration. It stands for the moment when God directly intervened into time and space to give us His Son. You don't get that kind of significance with a candy cane.

. . . IN THE SMALL STUFF

- Don't let God's presence be overshadowed by the Christmas presents.
- The decorations in your house aren't nearly as important as the spirit of Christmas in your heart.
- Whenever the story of God's love for humanity is explained, the story of Christmas is told.

"The Savior—yes, the Messiah, the Lord—
has been born tonight in Bethlehem,
the city of David!"
LUKE 2:11 NLT

= 94 =

THE COMING MESSIAH

There's something about anticipation that's hard to beat. When we anticipate something—especially something really big—we tend to build it up in our minds. Sometimes, our mental buildup reaches the point that the anticipated thing, event, or person has a hard time meeting our expectations. What a letdown when that thing, event, or person doesn't quite measure up to what we had in mind.

Imagine something or someone that you once anticipated—then multiply the level of anticipation by spreading it out over fourteen hundred years or so, with each year adding to the intensity of your expectation. Now you have some idea of what the Jews—God's chosen people—were expecting when they imagined what their "Messiah" would be like.

Throughout the Old Testament, God promised the Jews that He would deliver them from their problems by sending a king to establish God's Kingdom on earth. This deliverer was referred to as "the Messiah." Moses was a great deliverer, but he never had a kingdom. In fact, no leader of Israel had a great kingdom until David came along. As the "anointed one," David was a type of messiah (the word literally means "anointed one"), but he was not *the* Messiah. Thoughtful Jews understood that no human king could fulfill the high ideal of the Messiah, who would be God coming down to earth.

After David's great earthly kingdom came to an end, the prophets of Israel began endowing the anticipated Messiah with names that clearly placed Him beyond mere mortals. He would be "Wonderful Counselor, Mighty God, Everlasting Father, Prince of Peace" (Isaiah 9:6 NLT). Furthermore, the Messiah would be:

- A direct descendant of King David (Isaiah 11:1);
- Born in Bethlehem, David's own birthplace (Micah 5:2); and
- Born of a virgin (Isaiah 7:14).

So the stage was set, and the time was right for God to send the great Deliverer to rescue His people—and that's what God did. He sent Jesus, the Messiah, the Anointed One, who was a descendant of David (Luke 1:31–33), born in Bethlehem (Luke 2:4, 6–7) and born of a virgin (Matthew 1:18, 22–23). God even sent one of His personal messengers, an angel who proclaimed on that first Christmas Eve:

> *"I bring you good news of great joy for everyone! The savior—yes, the Messiah, the Lord—has been born tonight in Bethlehem, the city of David! And this is how you will recognize him: You will find a baby lying in a manger, wrapped snugly in strips of cloth!"*
>
> LUKE 2:10–12 NLT

There was no mistaking it. The prophecies had been fulfilled. God had come to earth in the person of Jesus. The Messiah had come. Surely the Jews would embrace their king.

There was only one problem. They were anticipating a different kind of Messiah, and the baby lying in the manger didn't measure up to their ideal. They expected a royal king born in a palace; what God sent them was a common baby born in a stable. They expected a birth announcement to be made to the religious leaders; God first told a bunch of lowly shepherds. They anticipated a conquering king who would deal with their enemies and rule politically; Jesus came to serve and to give His life for others.

It's easy to criticize the Jews for missing the real point and rejecting Jesus the Messiah. But before we do that, we need to look at ourselves and ask what kind of Deliverer we're looking for. Are we expecting Jesus to deliver us from our problems? Are we expecting Jesus to deliver us from our enemies? Are we expecting Jesus to deliver us from poverty and sickness? Jesus can do all of those things, but that's not why He came. More than anything else, Jesus the Messiah came to deliver us from our sins.

. . .IN THE SMALL STUFF

- There have been many "messiahs" throughout history, but only one Messiah.

- The true Messiah doesn't simply meet the expectations of those looking for deliverance. He exceeds them.

- Without the coming of the Messiah, there is no Christmas.

*[Faith] is the confident assurance that what
we hope for is going to happen. It is the
evidence of things we cannot yet see.*
HEBREWS 11:1 NLT

=95=

HOPE

Christmas is a season of hope and wonder, but not for the reasons you think:

- Most kids have a particular gift they hope for, and they wonder if they are going to get it.

- A wife has the hope that her husband will get her a romantic gift, but she realistically wonders what electrical appliance she'll receive from him.

- We all hope not to get another fruitcake from the relatives, and when it arrives, we wonder if they will recognize it later in the backyard garden as a decorative boulder.

In these contexts, *hope* is merely a form of wishing. But the true spirit of hope at Christmastime has a much deeper and richer meaning. The *hope of Christmas* denotes an expectation with certainty. Christmas hope is a confident assurance that something will happen. It is a hope that you can hang on to when the rest of life seems shaky.

Christmas hope is thousands of years old, rooted in the history of the Jews. God had promised them a Messiah who would be their deliverer. They relied on this hope when they were enslaved by Pharaoh in Egypt (about 1700 BC). The promise of the Messiah also sustained them during the invasion of Israel when many of them were taken captive and transported to Assyria (about 700 BC) and when Jerusalem was destroyed and the Jews were exiled to Babylon (about 600 BC). And, during the earthly lifetime of Jesus, with the Jews suffering under the tyranny of the Roman government, they anxiously waited for the Messiah to lead a political revolt.

The birth of Christ—what we celebrate as *Christmas*—was the fulfillment of God's promise to send a Messiah. But few people recognized it as that. Their oversight is understandable. They were expecting the arrival of a conquering hero. They didn't imagine that their Deliverer would come dressed in a diaper. They wanted to see Him standing tall, holding a sword in His outstretched hand. They weren't expecting an infant squirming in a hay-strewn feeding trough.

Even when He grew to be a man, few people recognized Jesus as the Messiah. The people wanted relief from

Roman oppression, but Christ told them how to be free from sin and guilt. They wanted financial prosperity, but Christ spoke of success in terms of being reconciled with God. They wanted political peace, but Jesus offered spiritual peace. He wasn't what they were looking for—but the fact remains that God delivered on His promise to send what they needed, whether they realized it or not.

Now, about two thousand years later, God is still in the promise-keeping business. The Bible contains promises that God has made and not forgotten:

- You can turn to Him in times of crisis;
- He will provide for you in times of need;
- He loves you as His own child.

Skeptics might say that these are empty promises—nothing more than wishful thinking. But the hope of Christmas proves the skeptics wrong. These are the promises of the same God who made good on His pledge to send a Messiah. The God who invaded earth with His presence on that first Christmas night to fulfill His promise is the same God who can fulfill His promises to you.

God has proven Himself to be reliable. He can be trusted. Though the difficulties of life might make you question God's faithfulness, He is a worthy recipient of your hope. Maybe that is one reason He's given us the hope of Christmas. It is a perennial reminder that God keeps His promises. And you can hang your hope on that.

- The birth of Jesus was God making good on His promises.
- Wishing is for Santa Claus; hope is for Christ.
- The hope of Christmas is the confident assurance that God is in control and knows what He's doing.

Mary responded, "I am the Lord's servant,
and I am willing to accept whatever he wants.
May everything you have said come true."
Luke 1:38 nlt

FAITH

If you would argue that the Christmas story requires a lot of faith, we would agree—but not for the reason you might think. If by "faith" you mean "blind faith"—because there's just no way to know for sure that the events on that first Christmas happened the way the Bible says they did—that's not what we mean. It doesn't take any more faith to believe the historic fact that Jesus was born than it does to believe the historic fact that George Washington crossed the Delaware River. In both cases we have reliable information based on trustworthy witnesses, giving us good reason to believe these events happened—even though we weren't there to see them ourselves.

On the other hand, if by "faith" you refer to the action

required on our part to act on what we know to be true, then we are on the same page.

You see, it's one thing to believe that Jesus was born on Christmas Day and quite another matter to live your life as if this were actually true. By way of example, think about an airplane. You can have faith that a certain airplane will fly, but until you actually get on board and demonstrate your confidence in the plane, your faith doesn't count for much. It isn't an active, living faith.

Now think about Christmas. Rather than simply believing Christmas is true, insert yourself into the story. Think what it would have been like to believe the events would actually happen—before they happened. Imagine yourself as Joseph or Mary, both of whom were asked by God's messenger to do something extraordinary and quite unbelievable: to have faith in God that His only Son—the Savior who was coming to take away the sins of the world—was going to be born through them. Keep in mind that this was before anything had happened. They were asked to trust God before there was any physical evidence.

What if Mary and Joseph had believed God without acting on their belief? What if they had not accepted the assignment God gave them? Because we know that God will always carry out His plans, it is certain He would have found two other people to get the job done.

Real faith—the kind that is so evident in the Christmas story—is more than knowledge about something. Real faith is about personally trusting God and believing that what He says is true, even before it happens. When we have that kind of faith, we have no choice but to respond to God's call on our lives the way Mary did:

> *"I am the Lord's servant, and I am willing to accept whatever he wants. May everything you have said come true."*
>
> LUKE 1:38 NLT

What is our faith worth if we don't trust God completely? When faced with a challenge or an opportunity to get on board with God, our natural tendency is to trust our own abilities and our own understanding of the situation. We don't want to act unless we're absolutely certain we can get the job done. But God will never use us if we take that approach. He wants us to trust Him with all our heart. He doesn't want us to depend on ourselves, but to seek His will in all we do.

If we do that, like Mary and Joseph and so many other great heroes of the faith have done, God promises to direct us in all we do—in the small stuff as well as the big—as He uses our work and our words for His glory.

. . .IN THE SMALL STUFF

- When you have faith, you have confident assurance that what you hope for is going to happen.
- When you have faith, you can believe in what you cannot see.
- There is no limit to what God can do with the person who has faith.

Joy to the world, the Lord is come!
Let earth receive her King;
Let every heart prepare Him room,
And Heaven and nature sing.
ISAAC WATTS

= 97 =

PREPARE HIM ROOM

Every Christmas it's the same. You remember what it was like last year when you ran yourself ragged trying to get everything done. There were dinners to plan; programs to attend; parades and bowl games to watch; friends to have over; relatives to visit; presents to buy, wrap, open, and return. It's not like you set a goal to be busy. It just ended up that way.

But when the season passed, you felt exhausted and ashamed that you had missed the real meaning of Christmas—so this year you decided that things would be different. You're not going to get caught up in the frenzy. . .but the squeeze is already beginning. Your calendar is starting to fill up, your lists are lengthening. It's all good, right? It's all important.

So why do you feel like there's something missing? Probably because something really is missing. Or should we say *someone* is missing. Someone named Jesus.

We're not saying that you've intentionally left Jesus out of Christmas. It's just happening, the way it does every year. Because of everything else you've crammed into your life during this sacred season, you literally have no room....

> *No room in your schedule*
> *No room for quiet and reflection*
> *No room for solitude*
> *No room in your resources*
> *No room for Jesus*

On that first Christmas night there was no room for Jesus in the village inn. Now, during this Christmas season, once again there is no room. Because you haven't left any room in your schedule, your thoughts, your resources, and your heart, there's no room for the One who is the reason for the season. At the very time of year that should belong to Him, you're letting Jesus know that He doesn't belong.

It's not the way you want it. We know that, because we've been right where you are—many times. It's embarrassing. It's discouraging. But you know what? It doesn't have to be this way. We can do better. You can do better. But how?

As the Christmas carol "Joy to the World" suggests,

giving Jesus room in our schedules, our thoughts, our resources, and our hearts doesn't happen on its own. It takes thoughtful preparation. It takes careful planning. It takes intentional thinking. It takes opening our hearts. In short, it takes our best efforts to move Jesus from the fringes to the center of our lives.

Maybe the secret to our preparing Him room lies in the way we view Jesus. If we see Him in that manger year after year, we're going to keep thinking of Him as a baby. But we can't leave Jesus there, all wrapped up in that little feeding trough. We need to unwrap Him and give Him the room He deserves by letting Him grow in our lives.

. . .IN THE SMALL STUFF

- No room in your schedule means no opportunity for Jesus to do something surprising in your life.
- No room for quiet and reflection means no chance for you to hear God's still, small voice in your thoughts.
- No room for Jesus means no way for you to truly appreciate Christmas.

"I bring you good news of great joy for everyone!"
Luke 2:10 NLT

= 98 =

JOY

A ngels are often referred to as "God's messengers" because that's what they do: they carry God's message to us humans. They aren't ordinary messengers, of course, and whenever we read about their messages and the method of delivery, we can only begin to imagine what it was like to really be "touched by an angel."

When the angel brought word of Jesus' birth to the shepherds, the poor guys were scared out of their tunics. The Bible simply says they were "terrified," primarily due to the incredible "radiance of the Lord's glory" that surrounded the angelic being. Not one to let the shepherds grovel in fear, the angel reassured them by saying, "Don't be afraid! I bring you good news that will bring great joy to all people." After a celestial choir concert, the shepherds, filled with the joy of the Lord, ran to see "this thing that has happened, which the Lord has told us about." And then they told everyone who would listen (and, we suspect, some who would not) the good news of what they had just seen.

Thus began the story of Jesus on earth. Thirty-three years later, after He had lived His remarkable life, after He was crucified and resurrected, the angel appeared again (we like to think it was the same angel, perhaps Gabriel, one of God's favorites), surrounded by the Lord's glory as before. Once again, he inspired fear among the mortals, this time two women. And as he had done with the shepherds, the angel reassured them by saying, "Don't be afraid! I know you are looking for Jesus, who was crucified. He isn't here! He has been raised from the dead, just as he said would happen" (Matthew 28:5–6 NLT). As the women left the angel and the empty tomb, they ran to tell others the good news of what they had seen. The Bible says, "They were very frightened but also filled with great joy" (Matthew 28:8 NLT).

Don't you find it interesting that in both of these accounts there are four elements:

- An angel, surrounded by God's glory, appeared to ordinary people;

- The people, due to the angel's glorious appearance, reacted with great fear;

- After being told they had nothing to be afraid of, the people were filled with great joy; and

- They couldn't wait to tell others what they had seen.

Like bookends on the earthly life of Christ, these parallel

accounts tell us exactly *how* and *why* God has given us His joy. The *how* is pretty easy to see. God gave us His joy when He sent Jesus to be born. And then He gave us His joy again when He raised Jesus from the dead.

More perplexing is the *why*. Why would God share His joy with those who had turned their backs on Him? For the answer, you have to go back to God's character. It is in the nature of God to love us and share Himself with us, and that includes His joy. Jesus is the absolute fullest expression of God's joy, and one of the reasons He came was to give us lives full of joy (John 10:10). When we obey Jesus and immerse ourselves in His love, He guarantees that our lives will be filled with joy. Jesus said, "Yes, your joy will overflow!" (John 15:11 NLT).

But God also gives us joy because that gives *Him* joy. As God's joy takes root in us, as we enjoy Him and give Him glory, the Bible says He rejoices in us with great gladness (Zephaniah 3:17).

Now there's a reason to soak up all that Christmas has to offer. It's full of joy. . .God's joy. As we celebrate God's love for us and respond to Him in joy, the reason for the season will become incredibly meaningful for us—in the small stuff as well as the big.

. . .IN THE SMALL STUFF

- Happiness is temporary; joy is everlasting.
- By its very nature, joy overflows. That's why it's impossible to keep joy to yourself.
- Just as the darkest hour comes before dawn, your joy will often follow a time of deep sadness.

Probably the reason we all go so haywire at
Christmastime with the endless unrestrained
and often silly buying of gifts is that we don't
quite know how to put our love into words.
HARLAN MILLER

= 99 =

GIFTS AND GIVING

The tradition of Christmastime gift giving didn't begin when Jesus was born. Mary and Joseph may have marked the occasion of Christ's first birthday, but it wasn't celebrated with a gift exchange among the relatives and neighbors. The entire Christmas gift thing came hundreds of years later—and it probably wasn't rooted in the Christian faith. But we can still attach a spiritual significance to our own customs of giving and receiving gifts at Christmastime.

God gave the gift of His Son to all humanity that first Christmas evening. In doing so, He established some principles of gift giving that provide good guidelines for us to follow:

- The gift was exactly what we needed. One technical term describes a Christmas gift that nobody wants: fruitcake. But the category also includes Aunt Kim's gift of souvenir ashtrays to her nonsmoking niece and nephew; a necktie for Grandpa who only wears polyester jogging suits; and the box of See's candy you gave your pastor's wife, not knowing she was diabetic. God's gift, though, was specifically and uniquely what the human race needed— it was a gift designed and intended to cure our sin virus. God could have given other nice gifts (like heat without humidity or broccoli that tastes like chocolate), but anything less than a sacrifice for our sins would have left us in desperate need.

- The gift wasn't what we were expecting. Often, a gift may meet a need, though it isn't what the recipient was hoping for. Just ask any teenager who gets socks for Christmas. Sure, you need things like socks and toilet paper, but no one puts them on their Christmas list. The same is true of the Jews in the first century (and all of humanity since, for that matter). They wanted a Messiah who would free them from Roman oppression, leading them into autonomy and prosperity. They weren't expecting a Messiah who would speak about the spiritual freedom that comes from an intimate relationship with God. That's exactly what those first-century Jews needed, but they had other things higher on their list. Still, God gave them what He knew would be best for them.

- A sacrifice was involved. There may be nothing more disappointing on Christmas morning than receiving a gift that reveals a lack of effort on the part of the giver. Just ask a wife whose husband presents a stapled-shut bag from the Gas-N-Go; inside she finds a tin of breath mints, an assortment of candy bars, windshield wiper replacement blades, and an incriminating receipt indicating the purchase was made twenty-seven minutes earlier. In contrast, the most meaningful gifts are those that involve an obvious sacrifice by the giver. Balmy weather and candy-flavored vegetables would have been easy for God to conjure up. Such gifts might have been enjoyed by humanity, but the gifts would not have involved even the slightest inconvenience on God's part. Instead, He chose to send His Son to earth, knowing that Christ would be tortured and put to a brutal death. As the Bible says, "There is no greater love than to lay down one's life for one's friends" (John 15:13 nlt).

As you make your Christmas-shopping decisions, keep these principles in mind. Let your love for the recipient be reflected by a gift that is uniquely appropriate for that person. Give a gift that shows you made a sacrifice, not necessarily in money but in effort and thoughtfulness. And, whatever you do, don't Christmas shop at the Gas-N-Go.

. . .IN THE SMALL STUFF

- A gift of your time and attention is more valuable than anything that can be wrapped.

- An inexpensive gift is irrelevant if the gift was thoughtfully chosen. A high price is meaningless if there was little thought involved.

- Your appreciation is the gift you give back in return for a gift you have received.

But to all who believed him and accepted him,
he gave the right to become children of God.
JOHN 1:12 NIV

= 100 =

RECEIVING

Christmas is the season of giving. No one needs to tell you that, because this time of year every store and nearly every broadcasting station reminds you constantly that it's time to shop for gifts. And if you happen to miss the commercial clues, some of your closest friends and family members are more than happy to provide you with a list of suggested items they would love to receive.

You probably don't mind those attempts to inspire your giving. The old saying, "It's better to give than to receive," really is true. Giving is fun. Giving is fulfilling. What isn't as fulfilling is *receiving* gifts. That's not to say it isn't enjoyable, because it is. Opening presents is a blast, but our enthusiasm for what lies beneath the wrapping paper can quickly die, usually for one of two reasons.

One, the gift can turn out to be much less than you thought it would be. If this happens, it's important to maintain your cheery mood, even though you've just received a pair of oven mitts from Aunt Rose. Enthusiasm can also wane when you get a gift that goes way beyond what you expected—especially if you were "exchanging" gifts with another person. Elation can quickly turn to embarrassment, even resentment, if the gift puts you in an awkward position, such as feeling like you don't deserve it.

The point is this: not only is it better to give than to receive, it's also easier. Receiving something—especially something you don't think you deserve—can be tough.

Perhaps you already know where we're going with this. It's one thing to receive a valuable earthly gift for which you feel unworthy. Imagine what it's like to receive a gift from heaven—a good and perfect gift—whose value is beyond measure. That's exactly what God asks us to do at Christmas, when we are reminded that He has given us the greatest gift of all, the gift of His Son. And just as an earthly gift can't be earned (otherwise it would be more like a bonus than a gift), neither can God's heavenly gift. It must be received.

Makes sense, doesn't it? At Christmas, what good is a gift left under the tree, unopened? It's pretty to look at, but it doesn't do any good. Only when you open and receive the gift does it serve the purpose for which it was intended.

Think about God's gift of Jesus for a minute. Have you "unwrapped" and received the Gift? Or have you left Him wrapped and lying in the manger, waiting for Christmas to pass so you can put Him away for another year? The apostle John, reflecting on the fact that Jesus was born into a world that did not receive Him, made the observation that *anyone* who receives the gift of life through God's Son would gain the right to become God's children—in effect adopted into God's eternal family as coheirs with Christ.

There's nothing we could possibly do to be worthy of receiving God's great gift—it's based completely on His grace. But receive it we must, and what better time than Christmas?

. . . In the Small Stuff

- Receiving a gift is essential to the giving.
- Giving a gift is an option; receiving a gift is not.
- If you've never received God's great Gift, there's no better time to do that than now.

ABOUT THE AUTHORS

Bruce Bickel is an attorney, but he hopes he doesn't stay that way. Bruce and his wife, Cheryl, live in the Seattle area.

Stan Jantz was involved in Christian retail for twenty-five years before venturing into marketing and publishing. Stan and his wife, Karin, live in Ventura County, California.

Bruce & Stan have cowritten more than fifty books, including the international bestseller *God Is in the Small Stuff.* Their passion is to present truth in a correct, clear, and casual manner that encourages people to connect in a meaningful way with the living God.

Be sure to check out Bruce & Stan's website: www.Christianity101online.com

Bruce & Stan are the cofounders of **ConversantLife.com**, a content and social media online experience designed to promote conversations about faith and culture. They encourage you to check out this site for stimulating blogs, videos, podcasts, and news.

If you have any questions or comments, you can connect with Bruce & Stan at:

info@Christianity101online.com